THE UNIVERSITY
OF BIRMINGHAM

Young People in Care and Criminal Behaviour

of related interest

Leaving Care
Throughcare and Aftercare in Scotland
Jo Dixon and Mike Stein
ISBN 1 84310 202 1

Fostering Adolescents
Elaine Farmer, Sue Moyers and Jo Lipscombe
ISBN 1 84310 227 7

Developing Good Practice in Children's Services
Edited by Vicky White and John Harris
ISBN 1 84310 150 5

Foster Children
Where They Go and How They Get On
Ian Sinclair, Claire Baker, Kate Wilson and Ian Gibbs
ISBN 1 84310 278 1

Just Schools
A Whole School Approach to Restorative Justice
Belinda Hopkins
Foreword and Introduction by Guy Masters
ISBN 1 84310 132 7

Children's Homes and School Exclusion
Redefining the Problem
Isabelle Brodie
ISBN 1 85302 943 2

Understanding and Supporting Children with Emotional and Behavioural Difficulties
Edited by Paul Cooper
ISBN 1 85302 666 2

Violence in Children and Adolescents
Edited by Ved Varma
ISBN 1 85302 344 2

Young People in Care and Criminal Behaviour

Claire Taylor

Foreword by David Smith

Jessica Kingsley Publishers
London and Philadelphia

First published in 2006
by Jessica Kingsley Publishers
116 Pentonville Road
London N1 9JB, UK
and
400 Market Street, Suite 400
Philadelphia, PA 19106, USA

www.jkp.com

Library of Congress Cataloging in Publication Data

Taylor, Claire, 1976-
  Young people in care and criminal behaviour / Claire Taylor.
    p. cm.
  Includes bibliographical references and index.
  ISBN-13: 978-1-84310-169-7 (pbk. : alk. paper)
  ISBN-10: 1-84310-169-6 (pbk. : alk. paper) 1. Youth—Institutional care—Great Britain. 2. Foster children—Great Britain. 3. Criminal behavior, Prediction of—Great Britain. 4. Juvenile delinquency—Great Britain. I. Title.
  HV1441.G7T39 2005
  362.73'2—dc22

                                          2005019375

British Library Cataloguing in Publication Data

A CIP catalogue record for this book is available from the British Library

ISBN-13: 978 1 84310 169 7
ISBN-10: 1 84310 169 6

Printed and Bound in Great Britain by
Athenaeum Press, Gateshead, Tyne and Wear

Contents

Part III Conclusion

List of tables

Acknowledgements

First, I would like to thank the ESRC for funding part of the work presented in this book.

So many people have helped me in different ways with the research presented here that it is impossible to list them all. However, I would like to express my warmest thanks to David Smith at Lancaster University for his invaluable guidance and encouragement throughout the research process.

Other members of staff at Lancaster helped me in numerous ways. I would particularly like to thank Keith Soothill, but also Carol Thomas, Ian Paylor and Sue Wise. I am very grateful to Barry Goldson from the University of Liverpool for his helpful comments on various aspects of the research. My appreciation also goes to the reviewers who commented on an earlier draft version of this book.

On a personal note, friends and family helped me in many ways throughout the research process, but I would especially like to thank Tom for his unwavering love and support.

I received a great deal of help in accessing potential interviewees for this study, from probation officers, prison officers, aftercare groups and carers. However, I am particularly grateful to the young people who agreed to participate in the research for their willingness to talk openly and freely about their lives. The experience of interviewing these individuals is something that will always stay with me. For the purposes of confidentiality their names must remain anonymous.

Foreword

This is a book that ought to be read not only by academics and researchers in the fields of child care and criminal careers, but also by those responsible for shaping child-care policy. It sheds new theoretical light on an important concept in studies of criminality and child development, and presents vivid and often moving empirical material on what it means to be a child 'in care'.

The central theoretical concept of the book is attachment, which, as Claire Taylor argues, has been used by criminologists and specialists in child care and development in different ways. The academic habit of staying within the reassuring boundaries of one's discipline has meant that until now there has been no productive dialogue between criminological control theorists, for whom attachment to others is a crucial element of the social bond, and child development specialists, for whom attachment is the key to a successful adult identity and indeed to psychological health. Taylor's interdisciplinary approach allows her to begin to make connections between the two fields of research that should help to produce advances in studies of the links between childhood experiences – and careers in care in particular – and later criminal careers.

While recognising, and amply illustrating, the ways in which negative experiences of care can contribute to subsequent criminal involvement, Claire Taylor is also concerned to argue that there is nothing inevitable about such a progression. The fact of having been in care (or, in contemporary language, been a 'looked-after' child) does not inevitably or inherently predict later criminal involvement. Instead, the quality of the experience of care is crucial, and if children and young people are allowed to develop attachments to caring adults there is no reason why having been in care should be associated with continuing delinquency or disadvantage. Taylor argues cogently against the pessimism and fatalism that have characterised much discussion of the care system, and rejects the self-fulfilling prophecies and stigmatising labelling that this perspective tends to promote. Instead she stresses the diversity of care careers, and explores what can be learned from positive as well as negative experiences of care.

Claire Taylor gives a cautious welcome to recent initiatives designed to improve the quality of care and the support provided to young people emerging from the care system. She is, however, fully aware of the problems of resources and implementation that lie between good legislative intentions and their translation into effective practice. She points to the need – if we are to take the rhetoric of joined-up policies seriously – to integrate youth justice policy and practice with the welfarist intentions of the care system. Here her own integration of criminological and child development perspectives provides an example that both youth justice workers and child practitioners could usefully follow: they have more to learn from each other than they may think. While the current official rhetoric encourages a sharp division between children in need and young offenders – the former to be cared for and protected, the latter punished and controlled – Claire Taylor reminds us that for many children and young people the distinction is an artificial one. It is to be hoped that her analysis and research find a wide and attentive readership, not least among those who can have some influence on the shape of future policy.

David Smith
Professor of Criminology, Lancaster University

Introduction

Background

This book is about the relationship between young people's experiences of public care and criminal behaviour, a topic that has received surprisingly little attention from child-care researchers and criminologists. The disproportionate number of young offenders who have been in local authority care is reproduced year after year in the prison statistics and has generally been taken as given. A recent study found that 41 per cent of children in custody had at some time in their lives been in care (Hazel *et al.* 2002). Meanwhile, figures on offending rates tell us that looked-after children are about three times more likely to be cautioned or convicted of an offence than their peers (DH 2003a). The story is a familiar one, and there has been little attempt to look beyond the statistics.

What is of central importance, and needs to be seriously addressed, is that looked-after children will not *necessarily, inevitably* and *obviously* fare worse and achieve less than all other young people. This represents one of the many commonsensical assumptions that requires unpacking and challenging in terms of the relationship between offending and experiences of care.

Young people in the care system have been subject to sustained policy interest in recent years. A commitment to improving the state of the care system has been clearly on the British government's agenda. This has occurred partly as a result of an acknowledgement of the very poor outcomes for some care-leavers and the realisation that the state has often been a very poor parent in the past. Policy responsibility for children in care in England has recently shifted from the Department of Health (DH) to the Department for Education and Skills (DfES) – a change that reflects an increasing recognition that the education of children in care must now become a priority.

However, the issue of reducing offending rates amongst looked-after children and care-leavers has not been subject to quite the same level of attention. This is perhaps because official discourse encourages a sharp distinction between 'troubled' and 'troublesome' children. Children in the care and criminal justice systems are often treated very differently, regardless of the fact that they may all be children in need. This book calls into question the link between care and criminal careers, and places this important topic under investigation.

Research themes and questions

Whilst recognising that some young people do enter care as known offenders or with a 'baggage of disadvantage', the research in this book sets out to explore how going into care might counter the effects of previously negative family experiences and protect against offending behaviour in the future. At the heart of the research are three key themes:

1. We should not accept the link between care and criminal careers without question, but should consider how care might be made a more positive experience. Which aspects of the care experience might promote social inclusion and help to reduce the disproportionate number of care-leavers who become part of the prison population?

2. Low expectations of young people in care amongst policy-makers and practitioners alike can lead to a self-fulfilling prophecy whereby young people feel that there is little point in trying to achieve. Such expectations can exacerbate the problems already faced by young people, and reinforce the likelihood that they will face social exclusion in the future. Yet a consistent finding in research is that, even with prolonged early negative experiences, there is a wide variation in outcomes amongst young people (Rutter, Giller and Hagell 1998). What are the mechanisms involved that enable certain individuals to be resilient in the face of previous adversity?

3. Developments in modern criminological thought have the potential to inform social work practice and provide a wider theoretical framework for research on local authority care. Such a wider frame of reference has traditionally been lacking in research on the care system (Berridge 1997).

This book draws on messages from research, current policy developments and theoretical insights from the fields of criminology and social work in order to address the themes and questions above. In addition, the first two themes are explored through an empirical study involving qualitative interviews with 39 young people who have been in care in England. A further research aim was to give a voice to young people with first-hand experience of the care system, and use their informed views and opinions to illuminate both positive and negative aspects of care. Extracts from young people's own stories are presented in Part II of the book, although all names have been changed and identifying features occasionally altered in order to preserve anonymity.

The interviews were intended to explore the diversity of care careers and the different pathways that young people may take between care and custody. However, it should be noted from the outset that this study does not have a particular focus on remand fostering, which specifically involves young people entering care on the basis of an alleged offence. The intention of the research was to consider the care experience in far more general terms, exploring how a welfare-based intervention may contribute to, or protect against, involvement in crime.

The research presented in this book focuses on a topic that has tended to be taken as given, rather than empirically explored. The general acceptance that disproportionate numbers of care-leavers will end up in prison parallels the generally low status attached to children in public care. Low expectations of, and public indifference to, young people in the care system are widespread. However, such views are dangerous and need to be challenged. Indeed, public ambivalence towards individuals in care has been highlighted as an important factor associated with child abuse in the residential sector (Colton 2002). Furthermore, the reliability of care-leavers' complaints in alleged cases of past abuse in care has recently come under scrutiny in the field of criminal law.

> The mere fact of being in care (without evidence of criminal behaviour) appears to be regarded by defence advocates as ammunition with which to discredit a witness, and this would not be a viable tactic if it were not thought to alienate the jury from the complainant. (Birch and Taylor 2003, p.832)

This book attempts to illuminate what it means for individuals to be a child in care, in order to challenge such negative views. Before outlining the structure of this book, it is important to make a brief point on the terminology used.

Terminology

Social services for children are provided under the Children Act 1989, which came into force in England and Wales in 1991. Under this Act a child is 'looked after' by a local authority if he or she is placed in its care by the court (for example, under a care order) or provided with accommodation by the authority's social services department for more than 24 hours. Looked-after children fall into three main groups, which are:

1. children who are accommodated under a voluntary agreement with their parents (Section 20)

2. children who are the subject of a care order

3. children who are compulsorily accommodated. This includes children on remand, committed for trial or detained and those subject to short-term emergency protection orders.

Care provision for looked-after children and young people includes:

- foster placements
- children's homes
- schools and associated homes and hostels
- placed with parents
- placed for adoption
- in lodgings or residential employment
- other (including secure units).

Although the Children Act 1989 introduced the term 'looked after' as a less stigmatising replacement for the term 'in care', the former tends mainly to be used in official circles. Many young people in the care of local authorities today still regard themselves as 'in care', and this term continues to dominate in the wider society. I use the terms 'in care' and 'looked after' interchangeably throughout this book to refer to children and young people, accommodated either voluntarily or compulsorily by local authorities, in any of the provisions listed above.

A map of the book

This book is divided into three parts, with Part I setting the scene and establishing a context for the empirical research that follows.

Chapter 1 explores themes from the literature relating to what we know about experiences of care and after. A distinction is made between commonsensical assumptions and research knowledge. Messages from research that have contributed to our understanding of the link between care and criminal careers are also considered.

Chapter 2 outlines the current policy climate, which is dynamic and changing rapidly. There is a critical examination of New Labour's two-pronged approach to protecting vulnerable children and preventing criminality. The implications of this approach for young people in care who break the law are explored and some disjointed policy assumptions are highlighted.

Chapter 3 also makes links between child care and criminal behaviour, but focuses on theoretical insights as opposed to policy developments. Through the central construct of attachment this chapter combines insights from the domains of child care and criminology in order to develop a theoretical framework to inform research on care. The chapter moves on to introduce the empirical research, explaining how the study was conducted in practice. There is a particular focus on methods of data collection and analysis, and some demographic data on the interviewees are presented.

Part II of the book is based on the experiences of the young people interviewed and provides a thematic presentation of key issues.

Chapter 4 explores the residential care experience, which has traditionally been a recurrent theme in offending behaviour. Children's homes, in particular, are strongly associated in the public mind with delinquent children. There is a consideration of how far the experiences of those interviewed relate to this taken-for-granted assumption.

Chapter 5 considers the development of secure attachments in the context of care. The potentially positive effects of developing meaningful attachments with carers are explored and I investigate the care conditions that may enable such relationships to develop. This chapter focuses particularly on the foster care experience and on the experiences of several young people who lived in long-term foster care.

Chapter 6 examines the educational experiences of young people in the study and considers how being in care may affect experiences at school. There is a particular focus on the way in which educational attainment and involvement in school life can promote young people's self-esteem and help to protect against involvement in crime. At the same time it is noted that school can be a particular source of difficulty for looked-after children and a place where the stigma attached to being in care may frequently manifest itself.

Chapter 7 documents the experiences of individuals after leaving care and the difficulties of coping with independence at an early age. The implications of the Children (Leaving Care) Act 2000 are explored in light of the experiences of the young people interviewed. How far can the new legislation fill the gaps in provision experienced by generations of care-leavers? Can the Act help to reduce the number of pathways that lead too many individuals out of care and into custody?

Part III presents the conclusions of the research.

Chapter 8 draws the book to a close and summarises some of the key findings. Recommendations for policy and practice are made and I consider some future priorities for research in this area.

Part I
Setting the Scene

Chapter 1

What do we know about experiences of care – and after?

Introduction

According to the most recent government figures, nearly 60,000 children and young people are currently in local authority care, representing 0.5 per cent of the total under-18 population in England (DH 2003b). Current trends reveal that the number of children entering care is in decline, but those already within the care system are staying longer. Preliminary results from a survey in 2003 suggest that the average child in care is costing Social Services £600 a week (DfES 2003a) (which amounts to over £35m a week for the total care population). In light of such figures, the extensive literature on various aspects of care seems to be justifiable. However, whilst certain themes in the literature have been swamped by research, other areas are left comparatively neglected.

Children's homes are one type of child-care provision on which there has been an extensive focus at certain periods of time, often in response to wider societal concerns. Following constant scandals of abuse in children's homes throughout the 1990s, the Department of Health commissioned a programme of studies to look afresh at the residential sector (see Davies *et al.* 1998). Research interest in foster care has also gained momentum in recent years, with particular concerns including the value of kinship care (Broad 2001) and the potential of long-term foster care to provide an alternative family life (Schofield 2003). Yet, despite the wealth of research evidence available, there is still a great deal that we do not know about various aspects of care. Particular groups of children in care remain comparatively neglected by research, for example girls, ethnic minorities, short stay cases and those with a disability.

We can make some convincing statements about the 'big picture' issues in relation to the care system, such as the number of children who go into care, their age and legal status. However, the actual details of certain aspects of the care experience remain hazy, and up until recently a great deal about the experience of being in care has been assumed. This is particularly so in terms of the relationship between experiences of care and criminal careers, a relationship that is frequently referred to (e.g. Graham and Bowling 1995), but has rarely been seriously addressed. This chapter aims to document what we know about experiences of care and after, whilst acknowledging the differences between what is actually known and what is in fact assumed.

The diversity of care careers

Children can be in care at any age but the most common age group is currently 10–15-year-olds, who accounted for 42 per cent of children in care at 31 March 2002. Whilst the majority of young people (about 66%) who enter care today will go into a foster placement, about 11 per cent are placed in children's homes and a further 11 per cent are placed with their parents (DH 2003b). Higher proportions of teenagers are admitted to residential care than is the case for children in care as a whole.

For those who spend a long period in care, it is not unusual to experience both foster and residential care. However, many children who enter care will only ever experience temporary, short-term placements. This book is particularly concerned with the minority who spend a considerable time in care.

In their research into child care in Fife, Bilson and Thorpe (1988, p.37) identified three distinct types of care career:

1. 'Early leavers' (who leave care within six weeks of entry).

2. 'Late leavers' (who leave care between weeks 7 and 52).

3. 'Stayers' (those who are still in care at the end of the year).

Young people who do spend longer in care tend to be less likely to return home permanently and are often more likely to experience multiple placements. In Shaw's (1998) survey of 2000 young people in care in the UK, 23 per cent had experienced only one placement, whilst 49 per cent had had between two and five. A minority of 11 per cent had experienced multiple placements of 11 or more. Clearly the experience of movement in care can be very disruptive for young people. Often it means losing contact with family, friends and former carers, and it may well require a change of school or college. Such instability in care is well recognised and appears to be an entrenched part of the system, although there are ongoing efforts to reduce this problem (DH 1999).

It is clear that there is a very diverse range of individual care careers. There is also a variety of experiences that children may bring with them into care (cf. DH 2003b). As Bullock (1990) has commented, although most children in care spend time away from home, they differ widely in many other respects, such as family background and reason for admission:

> While certain sub-groups of children can be identified, such as abused children or those beyond parental control, no single group dominates the total care population. Indeed children and families often find themselves stigmatised by groundless assumptions that because an admission to care has occurred, abuse or control must be an issue. (p.354)

Research on foster care

As the most 'popular' type of care provision accounting for the majority of looked-after children in England today, it is perhaps not surprising that foster care has been witness to sustained research interest in recent years. A recent scoping review of the literature in this area uncovered a wealth of material published from the year 2000 onwards (Wilson *et al.* 2004). It also identified a number of issues that were subject to dispute amongst researchers; for example, whether kinship or stranger foster care was preferable and the level of contact that foster children should have with their birth families. In addition, the review found the issue of effecting and conceptualising good outcomes in foster care to be extremely complex.

Minty (1999) argues that for many foster placements, success is judged on the criterion of whether or not a child returns home. This is because the commonest form of care is now short term, which is intended to last less than three months. However, evidence suggests that outcomes for long-term foster care may be better than is often assumed. Dumaret, Coppel-Batsch and Couraud (1997) found in their study of adult outcomes after long-term foster placements in France that 56 per cent of their sample were well integrated socially and had managed to overcome childhood adversity. A further 12 per cent had average integration results, whilst only 10 per cent were in situations of failure. In light of such work, Minty (1999) questions whether the current policy of short-term admissions to care is always in the child's best interests, as 'it may have encouraged the "oscillation" of children in and out of care, and the postponement of some long-term admissions' (p.997).

Similar concerns are expressed by Schofield *et al.* (2000), who argue that since long-term foster care exists it needs to be recognised and understood. They suggest that it is 'one of the best kept secrets of the child care system' (p.1), and certainly should not be regarded as a last resort, as such a view can lead to children remaining at home in maltreating families or drifting in and out of short-term care (see also Schofield 2003). Of course foster care may not be suitable for all children and young people who are looked after, which is why alternative types of care provision exist.

Residential care and secure accommodation

Early research on residential care focused particularly on approved schools and provision for difficult adolescents (e.g. Cornish and Clarke 1975; Dunlop 1974; Millham, Bullock and Cherret 1975; Polsky 1962), whilst placements such as children's homes received comparatively little attention (Bullock, Little and Millham 1993). A general disillusionment with the effects of residential care, particularly on delinquency, was evident in much of this work. Millham *et al.*'s (1975) research revealed that regime differences only accounted for a 10 per cent variation in re-offending rates, whilst Cornish and Clarke's (1975) findings led them to conclude that 'there is reason to guard against intervening in the life of the child or family' (p.50). A rapid decline in the use of residential care for children followed.

During the 1980s and 1990s residential care was plagued by constant scandals of physical and sexual abuse, which led many to conclude that the sector was in a state of crisis. A succession of government inquiries followed these scandals, in an attempt to ensure that such atrocities would not be allowed to happen again, (e.g. Utting 1991, 1997; Warner 1992). Most recently, Sir Ronald Waterhouse's £15m report on child abuse in North Wales exposed the terrible neglect of children in care homes in Clwyd and Gwynedd (Waterhouse 2000).

Despite the continued questions about the efficacy and cost of residential care, few disagree with Utting's (1991) conclusion that for some young people it represents an 'indispensable service' (p.62). For example, some individuals decide that they do not wish to be fostered, others have had bad experiences of foster family life and some require conditions of containment and help in security. Warwickshire is the only local authority in England that has attempted to do without any children's homes at all, and this experiment was found to be highly problematic (Cliffe and Berridge 1991).

Therefore, the Department of Health commissioned a programme of studies to look anew at the residential sector, presenting their findings in an overview publication entitled *Caring for Children Away From Home* (Davies *et al.* 1998). The researchers describe a blurring of the boundaries between residential and foster care for children, and note that the average children's home now has just seven residents. In addition, there is little to choose between the average length of stay in foster and residential homes. Davies *et al.* (1998) argue that 'on the whole it is better to keep the size of children's homes small and the ratio of staff to residents as low as possible [sic]' (p.23). Similar recommendations have been expressed elsewhere (e.g. Frost, Mills and Stein 1999; Sinclair and Gibbs 1998).

One particular type of residential care provision that often receives specific attention is local authority secure accommodation. Whilst certain forms of violence may prompt admission to secure care, some young people are admitted for reasons that have nothing to do with law breaking, such as self-harming. As Harris and Timms (1993) point out, secure accommodation is a custodial provision that attempts to deal with different categories of offender as well as non-offenders. In March 2003 there were 445 approved places in 31 secure units in England and Wales, 420 of which were filled (DfES 2003b). The number of young people in secure accommodation therefore represents less than 1 per cent of the total looked-after population, yet the issues surrounding locking children up are complex and a cause for concern.

The National Children's Bureau (1995) argues that dangerous children, children on remand and self-destructive children should not, as a general principle, be accommodated together. O'Neill's work (2001) highlights a further problem with secure accommodation. In her study she found that most of the boys, who form the majority of children locked up, were admitted through the criminal justice system. By contrast, the majority of girls were admitted through the welfare system. She argues that this makes the whole 'care versus control' debate a gendered issue, whereby girls in particular may end up receiving more control and punishment than they deserve.

More recently, Goldson (2002a) has asserted that secure units are becoming increasingly led by penal concerns. The implications of this for children placed in secure care on welfare grounds are clearly very worrying, and may prompt practitioners to look increasingly towards alternative provision (cf. Walker, Hill and Triseliotis 2002).

Public attitudes to care

Although secure accommodation is necessary, only a very small proportion of the total care population will ever need it and it is important to remember that young people may enter care for a variety of reasons (Bullock 1990). However, popular perceptions continually link children in care with trouble and there seems to be an entrenched stigma associated with entering the public care system. The term 'careism' was coined by Lindsay (1996) to describe the widespread discrimination against young people in care. Such discrimination is arguably a particular problem for young people in the residential sector. Kahan (1979) found that the 'children's home kids' tended to be regarded as outsiders by both staff and other pupils at school, a finding that has been frequently reiterated in later work (e.g. Morris 2000).

According to the Warner report (1992), 'Children's homes are strongly associated in the public mind with deprived and delinquent children. Dickensian images of 19th century orphanages still linger on' (p.11). In some respects this is still very much the case today. In the wake of the recent North Wales scandal and the subsequent government inquiry (Waterhouse 2000), there was relentless media attention and public disbelief over the horrific sex crimes that had been exposed. A key question asked was how such abuse could continue undetected for so long. One leading commentator, quoted in an article in the *Independent on Sunday*, explained the situation in the following way:

> The public perception was that they were children who were dangerous or delinquent and that was why they were in care. They were also not to be believed because the people they were making allegations against were very important members of staff. (Dobson 2000, p.16)

As Morris (2000) recognises, the 'common labelling of children in the care system as mad or bad' (p.3), as well as public attitudes towards children in general (the belief that children are inconsistent and untrustworthy), represent fundamental barriers to improving experiences of public care (cf. Colton 2002). Yet, working out how to change attitudes is no easy task.

Perceptions of stigma attributed to various public child welfare services in the Netherlands, Catalonia and Wales were studied by Scholte *et al.* (1999). They found that 'foster and residential care invoked the greatest sense of stigma amongst service users, while health-related and preventive services were more positively regarded' (p.388). The authors conclude that the placement of children in residential institutions and foster homes should be avoided where possible. This is in line with current thinking in Western child-care policies and practices that preventive and family-oriented welfare services should always be offered first (cf. Biehal, Clayden and Byford 2000, on adolescent support teams).

Educational achievement

It is of course possible to distinguish between positive and negative labelling (cf. Braithwaite 1989). The former, in the shape of compensatory education, has been suggested in relation to the education of young people in care, as many care-leavers have a low level of educational achievement. Heath, Colton and Aldgate (1994) found in their study that even foster children in long-term, settled placements were unable to 'escape from disadvantage' and fare well educationally.

In recent years there has been an explicit recognition that education is of crucial importance in enabling young people to be resilient in spite of previous disadvantage and adversity. A new guidance specifically addressing the education of young people in care was launched by the government in the year 2000 (DfEE and DH 2000). The first ever national statistics on the educational qualifications of care-leavers were also published in the same year, and revealed that 70 per cent of young people leaving care during 1999/2000 had no qualifications (DH 2000). It is noteworthy that this figure fell to 56 per cent in 2002/2003 (DfES 2003c).

Poor educational attainment may be problematic for a number of reasons, not least because it is a risk factor for offending behaviour. Longitudinal research has consistently shown that children who are performing poorly from late junior school onwards are more likely to become involved in crime and drug abuse than those performing adequately or well (Communities that Care 2001, p.13). There is also a clear link between truancy, school exclusion and offending behaviour (McCarthy, Laing and Walker 2004). The Market and Opinion Research International (MORI) Youth Survey found that 60 per cent of excluded young people have offended compared to 26 per cent of young people in mainstream education (MORI 2004).

In light of the evidence above, it is of concern that looked-after children are more likely than their peers to receive a permanent exclusion from school, and more likely to have a statement of special educational needs (DH 2003a). Of course some children may have difficulties at school before going into care. Indeed, prior experiences of poverty and deprivation amongst young people in care are associated with underachievement (see e.g. Borland *et al.* 1998). However, for other children, the care experience may create educational problems.

A report by the Social Exclusion Unit (SEU) on raising educational attainment has identified five key reasons why children in care may underachieve (SEU 2003, p.4).

- Too many young people's lives are characterised by instability.

- Young people in care spend too much time out of school or other places of learning.

- Children do not have sufficient help with their education if they get behind.

- Carers are not expected, or equipped, to provide sufficient support and encouragement at home.

- Children in care need more help with their emotional, mental or physical health and well-being.

The issue of instability in care has been highlighted as a particular problem in previous research (e.g. Goddard 2000), because frequent placement changes may result in frequent school changes. The low priority traditionally afforded to education by both residential care workers (Berridge and Brodie 1998) and social workers (Stein 1994) is an additional factor associated with low attainment. Whilst educational problems are sometimes associated with admission to care in the first place, research findings do suggest that the care experience has often done little to improve the situation for young people. In some cases it has simply compounded existing difficulties. This has led some to highlight the importance of building on the strengths of young people in care rather than continually dwelling on their problems (Jackson and Sachdev 2001).

A particularly interesting study that resists any assumption of a necessary correlation between being in care and low educational attainment is offered by Jackson and Martin (1998). They studied the experiences of 38 care-leavers who were regarded as high educational achievers, and identified a number of protective factors associated with academic success. These included stability and continuity, learning to read early and fluently, having a parent or carer who valued education and having friends outside care who did well at school (1998, p.578). Not surprisingly, educational attainment was also associated with more positive outcomes after leaving care.

Leaving care

This book deals with leaving care at the upper age limit, rather than leaving care to return home or to be adopted at a younger age. Virtually all of the literature on leaving care documents the difficulties faced by young care-leavers who, already vulnerable, are frequently forced into independence at an early age. Stein and Carey's seminal work *Leaving Care* (1986) was one of the first in-depth studies in this area to document the accounts of young people who had left the care system. It illustrated the frequency of experiences such as loneliness, isolation, movement and drift, unemployment and dependence on benefits.

Similar experiences were documented by Biehal *et al.* (1995) who found that many young people continued to leave care at 16 and 17 – much earlier than their peers left their family homes. Since this research was carried out, the Children (Leaving Care) Act 2000 (discussed further in Chapter 2) has finally placed a new duty on local authorities to assess and meet the needs of children aged 16 or 17 who are in care or care-leavers. There is also now a duty to provide support to 18–21-year-old care-leavers.

How far the new legislation will improve outcomes for young people after care is not yet clear. However, preliminary findings from the first national evaluation of the Act suggest that progress has been made by some leaving-care projects. This is particularly so in relation to identifying levels of need amongst young people and service planning, although not in terms of actual service provision (Broad 2003).

Whilst the introduction of the new Act is undoubtedly a positive step forward, what of those who have already left local authority care? The Social Services Inspectorate (1997) has summarised some of the particular difficulties faced by care-leavers. In addition to the fact that many lack any academic qualifications:

- More than 50 per cent of young people leaving care after 16 years are unemployed.

- 17 per cent of young women leaving care are pregnant or already mothers.

- 30 per cent of young single homeless people have been in care.

- 23 per cent of adult prisoners and 38 per cent of young prisoners have been in care.

In order to reduce the incidence of homelessness, unemployment and so forth, it is clear that care-leavers are a very important group to address and assist. One way to help improve outcomes after care is to examine the experiences of those with more positive outcomes. Placement stability (Jackson and Thomas 1999), educational attainment (Goddard 2000; Jackson and Martin 1998) and forming long-lasting relationships with carers (Schofield 2003) are all associated with the well-being of young people after care. Continued support from foster carers after young people have left care has been shown to be particularly important. Early preparation for independence, including help with budgeting, cooking and personal care, has also been identified as a crucial factor in enabling successful transitions (Stein 1997).

Having established that positive care experiences do exist, it is important that poor outcomes after care are never accepted as inevitable. With this in mind the remainder of this chapter focuses on one specific outcome that tends to be strongly associated with experiences of care.

The relationship between care and crime

Although popular perceptions connect care with trouble, many care-leavers have never had any involvement with the police. The relationship between care and crime is complex and requires more research (cf. Stein

1997). Interestingly, this relationship has often been assumed to exist, although there is little research that specifically addresses how care careers can lead to criminal careers and vice versa. However, it has been shown that those with a history of being in care are disproportionately involved in the criminal justice system and over-represented in the prison population (cf. Dodd and Hunter 1992).

The evidence that does exist on the connection between care and crime can be distinguished between data that focus on concurrent (youth) offending and data on subsequent (adult) offending. The most recent figures on youth offending reveal that looked-after children of the age of criminal responsibility are about three times more likely to be cautioned or convicted of an offence than their peers. In the year ending September 2002, 9.7 per cent of looked-after children in England received a caution or conviction, compared to 3.6 per cent of all children (DH 2003a). Focus group research with young offenders conducted for a Home Office study revealed that many had experienced disrupted lives, changing family relationships and long periods of time in the care system (Lyon, Dennison and Wilson 2000).

More recently a study by the Youth Justice Board showed that 41 per cent of children in custody had some history of being 'looked after' (Hazel *et al.* 2002). Of course this does not necessarily mean to say that similar proportions of a leaving-care cohort will go on to prison. Indeed, information collected for the first time in 2001/2002 on the location of care-leavers on their 19th birthday (i.e. those classed as adults), revealed that just 2 per cent (n=110) were in custody, the overwhelming majority of whom were male (DH 2003b). This figure clearly paints a very different picture from that provided by the Youth Justice Board study (Hazel *et al.* 2002).

However, given that only 0.5 per cent of the under-18 population are currently in care (DH 2003b), it seems that a disproportionate number of these young people will become involved with the criminal justice system at some point in their lives. This might lead us to expect that the majority of young people in care are admitted to care under criminal proceedings. Yet this is certainly not the case. Of the 24,600 children who started to be looked after during the year ending 31 March 2002, a mere 3 per cent were on remand, committed for trial or detained (DH 2003b). This figures moves up to 6 per cent when only children of the age of criminal responsibility are considered. (Naturally, an infant who becomes looked after will not be on remand.)

With regard to the principal reason for being looked after in the year ending 31 March 2002, 8 per cent of children were admitted to care because of 'socially unacceptable behaviour'. However, the largest category of need was 'abuse or neglect', which accounted for 44 per cent of children being admitted to care (DH 2003b). The remaining principal reasons were:

- absent parenting (10%)
- disability (3%)
- family dysfunction (14%)
- family in acute stress (12%)
- low income (1%)
- parental illness (9%).

Of course it is entirely possible that in cases where the principal reason for admission to care is something other than 'socially unacceptable behaviour', the young person in question may still be exhibiting such behaviour. However, if he or she is also being abused or neglected, for example, then this category of need will inevitably take priority. It is important to be aware that, in England and Wales, children under ten years of age are not regarded as criminally responsible and cannot go into custody. Therefore, the under-tens with a history of offending may be more likely to be admitted to care under a care order.

The majority of children and young people currently in care (64%) are subject to care orders, as opposed to being in care under a voluntary agreement (DH 2003b). The current criteria for care orders being made include cases where the child is considered 'beyond parental control'. Consequently, individuals may be placed under a care order if they are exhibiting antisocial behaviour, even if they have not yet committed, or been found guilty of, a criminal offence.

We could infer from all this that, whilst few individuals are actually admitted to care under criminal proceedings, many may enter care because they are already regarded as at risk of involvement in crime. Therefore, there will inevitably be a disproportionate number of looked-after children and care-leavers coming into contact with the criminal justice system. Yet this position implies that there is little possibility of redirecting antisocial pathways or diverting individuals from involvement in crime, a suggestion that is made untenable by criminological research (e.g. Sampson and Laub 1993).

An alternative explanation is that the care system is failing to have any positive impact at all on children and young people who enter care. Yet this position does not fit with the research evidence that illustrates that positive experiences in care and after care do exist (e.g. Dumaret *et al.* 1997; Jackson and Martin 1998). One thing we can be sure of is that the relationship between care and crime is complex, as messages from research suggest.

Research from the UK

What lessons can be learnt from research that does attempt to address the complex interaction between care and crime? Following the publication of Bowlby's *Forty-Four Juvenile Thieves* (1946) there have been various studies of the relationship between some form of 'maternal deprivation' and delinquency in boys (e.g. Rutter 1971). Some of the early research on residential care was particularly concerned with the effects of residential regimes on delinquents (Cornish and Clarke 1975; Dunlop 1974). In particular it was noted that placing delinquents together in an institutionalised setting may well result in their mutually reinforcing each other's delinquent tendencies and behaviour (Millham *et al.* 1975; Polsky 1962).

Certainly it seems that peer pressure and the development of deviant sub-cultures is a major difficulty for residential care, referred to by some as a 'socialising milieu' for delinquency (see Stewart *et al.* 1994). Yet much of the early research on residential care begins with young people who are already delinquent, those who would most probably have been committed to care. In trying to understand the variety of pathways between care and custody, it is important also to study the experiences of young people who are not known delinquents when they enter care. A small number of studies from Ferguson (1966) onwards have done this.

In *Child Care and Adult Crime*, Minty and Ashcroft (1987) set out specifically to examine outcomes after care in relation to criminal involvement. In this particular study, the one index of outcome used is convictions for indictable and other serious offences over the age of 16. The study compared the outcomes of children in care with the outcomes of children seen at child guidance clinics and chronic school non-attenders. Using local and criminal records, the researchers studied 300 children born between 1944 and 1953 who were brought up in an inner city area in the north of England.

Minty and Ashcroft (1987) found that over 90 per cent of boys admitted to care for reasons of delinquency, remand or being beyond control had convictions as adults. Yet the number of young men who had been admitted to care because their parents had died, been ill or were in other ways unable to cope, also had a disappointingly high number of convictions. Of this group, 41 per cent had three or more convictions in adulthood. One of the more significant findings in this study was that boys who stayed longest in care did relatively well, whilst a group of children admitted to care early in life who were later discharged home did very poorly.

On the basis of their results, the authors question the belief that living long term in care is inevitably damaging (cf. Minty 1999). They note that, although many people who have been in care at some point in their lives are subsequently involved in crime, 'it does not follow that their problems are necessarily as a result of having lived "in care"' (1987, p.29). In fact, as they rightly point out, many children who enter care are already considerably disadvantaged and it is not always easy to help them overcome the 'baggage of disadvantage' that they carry with them.

A further study that offers an excellent contribution to our understanding of the relationship between care and custody is provided by Pat Carlen. Carlen's (1987) analysis of the 'care factor' in criminal careers emerged as a result of a wider study she had undertaken on the causes and consequences of women's law-breaking. During her interviews with women who were, or had been, in penal custody, she discovered that 22 of the 39 women she spoke to had previously been in residential care. Whilst presented as only one part of a larger study, Carlen's (1987) analysis of care is nevertheless illuminating, particularly as it focuses exclusively on women, a group that has tended to be left in the background of previous studies.

In addition, Carlen's (1987) work provides an important qualitative focus in this area. Her interviews allow her to pursue individual accounts in depth, as well as enabling those who have actually been in care to give their comments and opinions. Carlen (1987) found that lack of preparation for non-institutional living was one of the major problems confronting young people leaving residential care. She pointed out that 'all the women stressed that anyone who had been in care could cope with prison' (p.157). As has been noted in the leaving-care literature, it is crucial that preparation for independence begins at an early stage (Stein 1997).

With regard to life in residential care, it is noteworthy that Sinclair and Gibbs (1998) recently found that 40 per cent of young people (n=674) with no cautions or convictions prior to entering care had one after six months or more of living in a children's home. Although this figure may include a small number of young people who were convicted of offences that were committed before their arrival in a home, the findings remain a serious cause for concern.

Finally, in their analysis of the Looking after Children longitudinal study of 249 looked-after children, Ward and Skuse (2001) found that, whilst 24 of those aged over ten for whom information was available (n=81) had a criminal conviction or caution at admission to care, a further 11 children had offended by the follow-up date. The authors note that 'young people who acquired a criminal record after admission were significantly more likely to have been living in a residential unit at some point during their care episode' (p.342).

Research from the USA

Interestingly, recent research in America has considered the issue of out-of-home placements and crime in the context of wider debates about the factors that may contribute to, or protect against, criminal careers. Using data from the California foster care records, Jonson-Reid and Barth (2000) explored the likelihood of adolescent incarceration for serious and violent offences among children with a history of foster or group care placement. Although just 0.75 per cent (590) of their final sample (n=79,139) ended up in the California Youth Authority (CYA) – the state-wide system designed to house the most serious youthful offenders – the authors identified a number of risk factors associated with CYA entry. They found that children first placed between the ages of 12 and 15, children with multiple placements and children with multiple spells in care had a higher risk of incarceration for a serious or violent offence during adolescence. An increase in risk was particularly apparent for those entering care three or more times.

Johnson-Reid and Barth (2000) also found that females within the child welfare system faced particularly high levels of risk for adolescent incarceration when compared to females in the general child and youth population. As the authors note, this does not necessarily mean that child welfare services are causing poor outcomes for females. Rather, there are serious gaps in our understanding of how males and females differ in their response to maltreatment and service experiences (cf. Farrington and Painter 2004). Gender differences in placement outcomes were also reported by McMahon and Clay-Warner (2002). They found that an out-of-home placement reduced the likelihood of adult arrest for males who had experienced frequent family moves (residential mobility), yet increased the risk of arrest for females. Clearly, such findings warrant further exploration.

Another notable contribution from the USA has been provided by researchers in Michigan. Collins, Schwartz and Epstein (2001) examined five cohorts of male youth released from a residential home for troubled youth in Michigan (n=1550) to determine the likelihood that they would later appear in the adult correctional system. They found that approximately one quarter of the youth studied were sentenced to adult corrections within seven and a half years of release. According to the authors:

> Of significant concern is the finding that the risk of sentencing did not differ depending on whether a youth was placed at Boysville for committing delinquent acts or whether he was there due to dependency, abuse, or committing a status offence. Moreover, analysis of offence type found a significant percentage of non-delinquent youth were later sentenced for committing violent offences. (p.223)

Collins *et al.* (2001) question why non-delinquent youth ended up in the adult correctional system at a similar rate to delinquent youth. On the basis of their findings, they argue that placements in institutional settings such as Boysville limit the ability of youths to develop the type of life skills needed to make a successful transition to adult life. In their view, non-delinquent youths also suffer from being denied access to positive transition opportunities when they are placed in residential care.

The studies described above reveal some interesting insights about the connection between care and crime, but also raise important questions that have yet to be fully answered. For example, different gender responses to experiences of care clearly require further attention, as does the timing of first involvement in crime amongst young people who have lived away from home.

Conclusion

At the beginning of the chapter it was documented that there is a difference between what we actually know about experiences of care and what is in fact assumed. It has been argued that the relationship between care and criminal careers has not only been comparatively neglected in the literature but is also often assumed to exist regardless of how much we actually know about the topic. Even in the current political climate, where care is high on the political agenda, there is still 'a common labelling of children in the care system as mad or bad' (Morris 2000, p.3). Yet as Bullock (1990) points out, individual care careers are incredibly diverse. If experiences of care are ever to be made more positive, it is crucial that the stigma associated with care is broken down.

Recent research on the care system is very much concerned with improving outcomes for children and young people and has concentrated particularly on the importance of education (Jackson and Martin 1998; SEU 2003), placement stability (Jackson and Thomas 1999; Minty 1999) and continued support for care-leavers (Broad 1998; Stein 1997). These studies are all welcome additions to the growing literature on care and indicate important themes that ought to be examined in any study of care experiences.

However, the connection between care and offending behaviour, which is arguably at the heart of the stigma attached to care, has received relatively little attention. In light of the current research emphasis on improving outcomes after care, any attempt to analyse the relationship between care and crime seems to be a complementary exercise. It is time to question whether popular perceptions that link care with crime are justifiable or whether they serve to stigmatise an already vulnerable population. The following chapter considers the current policy climate in which this investigation takes place.

Chapter 2

The current policy climate

Introduction

The situation of children and young people in the care system has been high on the political agenda in recent years, leading some to suggest that the present climate is one of unprecedented government attention towards those in care (Morris 2000). This attention has been attributable, in part, to the scandalous tales of abuse experienced by individuals in care that were exposed throughout the 1990s (see, for example, Utting 1991, 1997; Waterhouse 2000). In addition, recent policies relating to young people in care are also clearly part of New Labour's wider strategy for tackling social exclusion.

Concern over the protection of children, the state of the care system and the poor outcomes for many care-leavers have resulted in the development of some positive initiatives such as the Quality Protects programme in England (DH 1998a). However, at the same time, the government has introduced various crime policies that have particularly harsh consequences for young people who break the law. Indeed, evidence suggests that custodial responses to children in trouble have been increasingly relied upon (Goldson and Peters 2000). Given that young people in care are three times more likely to receive a caution or conviction than their peers (DH 2001a), it seems reasonable to assume that the new youth justice provisions will have a disproportionate impact upon them.

This chapter aims to explore New Labour's two-pronged approach to protecting children and preventing criminality, which has arguably resulted in a series of incoherent and contradictory policy assumptions that are particularly likely to impact upon young people in care. What are the implications of the current climate for young people in the care system, who may be in need of varying degrees of both care and control? The discussion begins with a brief outline of the social exclusion agenda.

Tackling social exclusion

Since coming to power in 1997, tackling social exclusion has been one of the New Labour government's key concerns. During this time, there has been an emphasis on creating 'joined-up' solutions to what is essentially regarded as a joined-up problem.

> The 'joined-up' nature of social problems is one of the key factors underlying the concept of social exclusion... It includes low income, but is broader and focuses on the link between problems such as, for example, unemployment, poor skills, high crime, poor housing and family breakdown. Only when these links are properly understood and addressed will policies really be effective. (SEU 2001, s.4)

Reports from the Social Exclusion Unit (SEU) have highlighted that young people who have been in care are particularly vulnerable to various factors associated with social exclusion, such as truancy (SEU 1998) and low educational attainment (SEU 2003). Such evidence has encouraged a commitment in government to improving outcomes for young people in care.

However, there has also been a concern with early intervention into the lives of children and families considered to be at risk of social exclusion in the future (DfES 2003d). For example, the Sure Start programme works with pre-school children and their parents to promote the physical, social and emotional development of babies and young children – particularly those from disadvantaged areas. Sure Start has potentially positive implications; it is voluntary and aims to be supportive and non-stigmatising. Its long-term aim is arguably to reduce the need for future state intervention by the care and criminal justice systems. A similar initiative – On Track – is a long-term programme aimed at children at risk of getting involved in crime.

There are thought to be over 50 different government initiatives currently running in relation to tackling social exclusion and child poverty (George 2002). These initiatives are associated with a wide range of government departments. For example, the Connexions service, which was launched in 2000, is a multi-agency support service for children and young people aged 13–19. The service is intended to offer support and guidance to all teenagers through a network of personal advisers, something that may be particularly beneficial to young people in care. As a universal service, Connexions also has the advantage of being non-stigmatising.

In August 2000, the Children and Young People's Unit (CYPU) was established and given the task of coordinating the range of cross-government initiatives on child poverty and social justice. Whilst the criticism has been made that the fixed-term funding formulae of many of the government's initiatives could hinder the provision of sustained, long-term support (cf. Land 2002), it is worth pointing out that Sure Start, Connexions and the new CYPU are intended to represent policy developments that will endure.

A further criticism of the government's wider social exclusion agenda is that, despite some of the positive initiatives described above, a 'deserving–undeserving schism' (Goldson 2002b, p.683) has been evident in current policy, whereby there are harsher penalties for those who remain on the margins of society. For example, children who step out of line tend to be feared and harshly treated.

A key strategy adopted by the government is their 'rights and responsibilities' approach that makes state help available, but requires a contribution from the individual and family (SEU 2001). Consequently, under the New Deal benefits can be withdrawn if people do not take up opportunities and Educational Maintenance Allowances are conditional on attendance and performance. Certainly a degree of control is being imposed upon those who may need state support, as individuals and families are required to conform to what is expected of them in order to receive state welfare.

This outline of the current social exclusion agenda sets the scene for some of the later discussion. A brief review of legislation relating to child welfare and protection now follows.

Child welfare and protection

The Children Act 1989 states that the child's welfare should be the *paramount* consideration in court proceedings relating to a child's upbringing (s.1). Under Section 31, the grounds for care proceedings include *likely* significant harm to the child, as well as harm already inflicted. Although the Act is predominantly a welfare-based piece of legislation, it also addresses issues relating to the control of children. For example, under the legislation it is no longer possible to make a care order on the grounds of criminal proceedings. However, individuals may be placed on a care order if they are considered to be 'beyond parental control'. As noted above, care proceedings can be made when a child is regarded as at risk of *likely* significant harm. In this context, 'harm' may include being considered at risk of committing a criminal offence.

One of the most controversial types of provision for children and young people provided under the Children Act 1989 is local authority secure accommodation. This is arguably where the principles of welfare and justice truly converge (O'Neill 2001). In restricting the liberty of both disturbed and deviant children, secure accommodation attempts to meet the needs of both those in the care system whose needs are too extreme to be met by any other provision, and those in the criminal justice system who are regarded as 'vulnerable' in some way (Harris and Timms 1993). Worryingly, evidence suggests that secure accommodation is becoming increasingly led by penal concerns, and has severely limited procedures for safeguarding children's rights (Goldson 2002a).

Under the Children Act 1989, the rights of children and young people in care include the right to an independent visitor, the right to complain, the right to have their views heard and the right to contact with family and friends; although, as Morris (2000) points out, the human rights of children have not always been the dominant concern of social services departments. This is in spite of the development of various rights-based frameworks in the wider society. One such framework is provided by the UN Convention on the Rights of the Child, which entered into force in the UK in 1992.

Some of the key principles of the Convention are that:

- All rights apply to children without exception or discrimination of any kind (Article 2).

- The best interests of the child must be a primary consideration in all actions concerning children (Article 3).

- Children's views must be taken into account in all matters affecting them (Article 12).

More recently, the UK has introduced its own legislation in accordance with the European Convention on Human Rights. The Human Rights Act 1998 came into effect in the UK in October 2000 and provides additional support to protect children from unacceptable behaviour and abuse (Lord Chancellor's Department 1999).

In addition to wider social concerns over both human and children's rights, there has been a particular focus in recent years on the need to protect, and safeguard the welfare of, young people in the care system. The Children's Safeguards Review (Utting 1997) was particularly influential on the development of the government's Quality Protects programme, which aims to improve the experiences of looked-after children.

Proposals for a Children's Commissioner for Wales, which were set out in the Waterhouse report (2000), became statute under the Care Standards Act 2000. The Care Standards Act also establishes a National Care Standards Commission, an independent regulatory body for certain 'care services' in England. Meanwhile, the Protection of Children Act 1999 establishes the framework of a cross-sector system for identifying people unsuitable to work with children. Other recent developments include the appointment of the first Children's Minister for England in June 2003 and the development of new National Minimum Standards and Regulations for children's homes (DH 2002a) and fostering services (DH 2002b). In addition, under the new national advocacy standards for England (DH 2002c), children will have a legal right to choose an advocate if they have a concern or problem, or want to make a complaint.

Whilst the measures outlined above are undoubtedly positive steps in the right direction, it is important to recognise that there is a great deal of ground to be made up, particularly within the residential care sector. Colton (2002) notes that:

> services for our most vulnerable children are beset by problems of quite awesome magnitude, they are a national disgrace, and do not even approximate the standards to which any civilised nation should aspire and which exist in other European countries. (p.43)

In other words, any improvements to the residential sector begin from a very low base.

It is noteworthy that it is not only abuses in residential care that have received attention in recent times. Private fostering arrangements have also come under scrutiny following the death of eight-year-old Victoria Climbie in 2000, at the hands of her great aunt, Marie Therese Kouao, and Kouao's boyfriend Carl Manning. The independent inquiry into Victoria's death (Laming 2003) exposed a complete breakdown in the multi-agency child protection system and revealed that child protection staff missed many opportunities to save Victoria.

Partly as a response to the failures identified in the Climbie Inquiry, the government published a long-awaited Green Paper on children at risk in 2003, entitled *Every Child Matters* (DfES 2003d). A range of measures is outlined that is intended to improve the lives of all children. Proposals for new Children's Trusts are intended to help achieve the integration of frontline service provision through co-located services and multi-disciplinary teams of social services, health and education professionals.

Other measures include the appointment of an independent Children's Commissioner for England and a national campaign to recruit and retain more foster carers. It is noteworthy that increasing the number of carers available, and therefore placement choice, has also been an issue of concern under the Quality Protects programme.

Quality Protects

The government's Quality Protects programme (DH 1998a) was launched in September 1998 as the main vehicle for delivering the aims set out in the White Paper *Modernising Social Services* (DH 1998b). The overall aim of Quality Protects is to transform children's social services, focusing particularly on effective protection, better quality care and improving life chances. Within the programme, individual project teams are involved in exploring a range of issues concerning the care experience. These issues include child protection, leaving care, health and education, and also reducing offending. There is also a focus on particular groups of children, such as those with disabilities and those from black and minority ethnic backgrounds.

One topic that has received significant attention since the programme's launch is education, as it is well known that when a young person enters the care system, his or her education may be disrupted (cf. Goddard 2000). The finalised *Guidance on the Education of Children and Young People in Public Care* was published in May 2000 (DfEE and DH 2000) and contained a number of new measures. There are now specific time limits within which local authorities must secure educational placements for children and young people in their care. Furthermore, under the Guidance, schools are required to appoint designated teachers to act as a resource and advocate for looked-after children. These teachers will be required to liaise with Social Services on behalf of children.

In light of the fact that education has often been afforded a low priority by both residential care workers (Berridge and Brodie 1998) and social workers (Stein 1994), these new developments are certainly very encouraging. However, designated teachers will need to ensure that their very existence does not stigmatise looked-after children at school. Broadly speaking, the measures outlined above have been welcomed by groups concerned with the welfare of children in care. Despite initially setting an insultingly low educational target for looked-after children (that 50% achieve one GCSE or GNVQ when they leave school), there has been an important recognition in government that we need to raise expectations of children in the care system.

> Research has identified that those involved in corporate parenting have lower aspirations for, and expectations of, young people in public care, both in terms of achievement and behaviour. This stems from well-intentioned assumptions that children who have endured traumatic events in their lives simply cannot take advantage of learning opportunities... This government is committed to raising standards for all children. Higher expectations of children in public care, and of service providers in supporting them, are essential. (DfEE and DH 2000, s.4.11)

The last sentence above highlights a very important point; one that is emphasised in the SEU report on raising the educational attainment of children in care (SEU 2003). This report also outlines a new educational target – that at least 15 per cent of young people in care achieve the equivalent of five GCSEs graded A*–C by the year 2006, and that the proportion of those achieving this level of qualifications increases on average by four percentage points each year from 2002.

At the time of writing, the Quality Protects programme is in its last year and soon to come to an end. This raises the question of whether the progress made under Quality Protects can be sustained in the long term. However, it is anticipated that some of the work from this programme will be taken forward; for example, through new initiatives such as Choice Protects, which are intended to specifically improve fostering services and the choice of placements available to young people (DH 2002d).

The Children (Leaving Care) Act 2000

One particularly significant piece of legislation to emerge since the introduction of Quality Protects is the Children (Leaving Care) Act 2000, which came into force in October 2001. Under Section 24 of the Children Act 1989, local authorities had the 'power to assist' care-leavers up until the age of 21, a power that had been available to them since the Children Act of 1948! Yet research consistently highlighted the fact that many young people were still expected to leave care and cope on their own with minimal support at an age when most adolescents were living at home with their parents (Broad 1998).

The Children (Leaving Care) Act 2000 finally amends Section 24 of the 1989 Act and places a new duty on local authorities to assess and meet the needs of eligible children aged 16 or 17 who are in care or care-leavers. Wherever the young care-leaver lives, the local authority will have a duty to keep in touch with him or her until he or she is at least 21 years old. Also, the Act requires that all eligible 16-year-olds must have a Pathway Plan, mapping out a clear route to independence. A Young Person's Adviser will help young people to draw up their Pathway Plans and implement them. When the young person leaves care, the Young Person's Adviser will be responsible for keeping in touch until the young person reaches at least the age of 21, ensuring that the young person receives the advice and support to which he or she is entitled.

The Act also introduces a new financial regime in order to ensure that care-leavers have comprehensive support. As local authorities will be responsible for assessing and meeting the needs of 16- and 17-year-olds, these young people will no longer be eligible for welfare benefits. The aim of this measure is to simplify the situation for care-leavers, yet young people are unable to opt out of this new system other than in exceptional circumstances. Exceptions include lone parents and disabled children who would be able to claim benefits even if they were living at home.

A potential difficulty with this new regime is that the government has not set any minimum financial standard that care-leavers can expect to receive. This could cause problems for care-leavers who are estranged from their local authority. There is also the question of whether financial support will be dependent on compliance with the Pathway Plan. The relationship between young people in care and Social Services is often a tenuous one; in such cases the Young Person's Adviser may play an extremely important role.

Furthermore, although it is positive to note that the needs of care-leavers have at long last received some attention, the Act could have gone much further with its duties to older care-leavers. Under the Act, the responsible authority's duty to provide accommodation and mainte-nance for care-leavers ends when they reach the age of 18 (although care-leavers are identified as having automatic priority need for housing under the Homelessness Act 2002). However, local authorities do now have duties to care-leavers aged between 18 and 21 to provide general assistance and assistance with the expenses associated with employment, education and training. In addition, there is a duty to provide vacation accommodation (or the funds to secure it) to *all* care-leavers aged 16 and over in higher education or residential further education.

The new duties upon local authorities are undoubtedly a positive step forward and the focus on planning for independence and the future has the potential to be of significant benefit. However, although the Act emphasises that young people in education and employment will be entitled to additional assistance, it does not provide a duty to accommo-date them once they reach 18. Presumably many young people's Pathway Plans will be helping them to move out of care just as they are doing their A-levels or other college courses. This kind of disruption is hardly helpful to a population who, generally speaking, may require exceptional educational support in order to catch up with their peers (cf. Heath *et al.* 1994).

A further issue that requires consideration is the housing available to young people leaving care. Given that local authorities now have a duty to accommodate 16- and 17-year-olds in care and care-leavers, they may find themselves faced with a shortage of suitable housing provision. Although many young people want fostering or highly supported lodgings before moving to more independent accommodation, these resources appear to be in short supply (Social Services Inspectorate 1997). As for independent accommodation, we also know that there is a lack of available and affordable provision for young people in general.

Youth homelessness remains a pervasive problem in Britain, and one to which care-leavers may find themselves particularly vulnerable (Biehal and Wade 1999). Indeed, the lack of appropriate and affordable housing is one significant explanation for the increased incidence of extended youth transitions to adulthood in the general population (Coles, Rugg and Seavers 1999). This has resulted in young people remaining in the parental home for longer periods of time. In light of this trend, young people required to leave care at 18 under the new Leaving Care Act will continue to experience compressed and accelerated transitions to adulthood in comparison to many of their peers.

An important development, however, is that the vulnerability of care-leavers has been recognised in the new Homelessness Act 2002. Under the Act, care-leavers aged 18, 19 or 20 years who were looked after, accommodated or fostered when aged 16 or 17 are now identified as having automatic priority need. Local housing authorities now have a duty to provide accommodation to such individuals on an ongoing basis until more settled housing can be found.

The new legislation is clearly aimed at reducing the likelihood of care-leavers experiencing poverty, unemployment and homelessness – all of which may increase an individual's vulnerability to involvement in crime. Yet what of those who do offend and come into contact with the justice system? Whilst the issue of children's welfare and protection is currently high on the political agenda, concern over how to deal effectively with young offenders has resulted in the introduction of some particularly punitive measures. Consequently more and more young people have been serving custodial sentences in recent years.

Youth justice

According to official prison statistics (Home Office 2003a), the sentenced young offender population has increased by 50 per cent since 1991. With the exception of 1999, there have been year-on-year increases since 1993. At mid-2001, 1980 young offenders aged 17 or less were under sentence, a rise of nearly 6 per cent on the previous year (Home Office 2003a). Since the early 1990s, increasing numbers of children and young people have been locked up and trends suggest that young women in particular have been subject to greater criminalisation (cf. Worrall 2001). Since 1991 the female prison population (including adult and young offenders) has more than doubled (Home Office 2003a).

Worryingly, steep rises in the prison population have continued regardless of widespread concerns about prison overcrowding and overstretched budgets (Hough, Jacobson and Millie 2003). Moreover, the routine detention of children cannot be adequately justified by changing patterns of youth offending, because youth crime has been falling (NACRO 2003a). There appears to be a discrepancy between the alarming trends in the use of youth custody and the government's stated commitment to reducing the use of custodial provision for children (Children and Young People's Unit 2001).

In relation to young offenders, the New Labour government has placed a particular emphasis on the importance of parental responsibility. In November 1998 the Home Office published *Supporting Families,* its first ever Consultation Paper on the family. The document described juvenile offending as a serious family problem and noted that children who grow up in stable, successful families are less likely to become involved in offending. In the same year, the Crime and Disorder Act 1998 introduced a range of controversial new measures, including anti-social behaviour orders, parenting orders, child safety orders and child curfew schemes. In addition, the Act replaced the old secure training order with a detention and training order, which came into force in April 2000 and can potentially be applied to children as young as ten years old.

Perhaps the most controversial measure under the Crime and Disorder Act was the abolition of the fourteenth-century *doli incapax* principle, which was based on the assumption that children between 10 and 13 years of age were incapable of criminal intent. The presumption now is that children as young as ten are fully capable of understanding the consequences of their actions and are therefore criminally responsible in the same way as adults. As Goldson and Peters (2000) point out, not only do we lock up more children and young people than almost any other country in western Europe, we also have one of the lowest ages of criminal responsibility. The UK government was criticised on this very issue in a report compiled by the United Nations Committee on the Rights of the Child (UNCRC) (2002).

In its report the UNCRC also expressed grave concern about the fact that increasing numbers of children in the UK were being placed in custody for lesser offences and longer periods of time. This is in breach of Article 37 of the Convention on the Rights of the Child, which states that children should be locked up only as a last resort and for the shortest appropriate time. So how does the administration of youth justice in the UK fit with other legislation that emphasises the care and protection of children? In brief, once a child has committed a criminal offence, the rights afforded to him or her under welfare-based frameworks may be superseded by criminal justice legislation.

One important development is that a landmark ruling in the High Court in November 2002 finally placed an obligation on the government to apply the principles of the Children Act 1989 to children in Prison Service establishments (see Dyer 2002). This ruling is certainly to be welcomed. Furthermore, it is important to note that the Youth Justice Board (YJB) has expressed a commitment to reducing the use of custody for young people by ensuring that community penalties, such as Intensive Supervision and Surveillance Programmes (ISSPs), are seen as viable alternatives. The YJB has also expressed a commitment to the development of restorative justice (Youth Justice Board 2003a). Restorative practices are in fact evident in certain youth justice measures. For example, the referral order introduced under the Youth Justice and Criminal Evidence Act 1999 enables offenders to make amends for their behaviour to victims and/or the wider community.

Yet despite some encouraging signs, there remains in current policy an unrealistic dichotomy between children in need of care and protection and children in need of control. This is despite the fact that children in trouble are often those in need of the greatest care and attention.

The multiple forms of disadvantage experienced by young offenders are well documented in the literature (e.g. Haines and Drakeford 1998). As Smith (1999) notes, 'every study of the personal and social experiences of persistent known "offenders" reveals that almost all of them have endured various kinds of abuse, neglect, deprivation and misfortune' (p.159). Indeed, many of the risk factors associated with criminality, such as economic deprivation, parental mishandling, family criminality and school failure (Farrington 1986) are also risk factors associated with admission to care. Whilst the government has been criticised for being 'tough on the easiest of targets' (Butler and Drakeford 2001, p.124), there has also been wide condemnation of the conditions experienced by many young people in custody.

A report by the Howard League (1995), *Banged Up, Beaten Up, Cutting Up*, was particularly graphic in describing the terrible conditions experienced by some young offenders. Damning reports of certain young offender institutions by successive chief inspectors of prisons have also exposed neglect and unacceptable standards of care (e.g. Her Majesty's Chief Inspector of Prisons 1999). Certainly the occurrence of violence, bullying and self-harm in many penal settings is fairly well documented. As Goldson (2001) points out, 'we are literally awash with evidence which confirms time and time again that youth custody is corrosive, damaging, expensive and spectacularly counter-productive' (p.79). Although recent government proposals highlight the need to consider how to improve the protection of children who are locked up (Home Office 2003b), custody rates for young people continue to be of great concern.

The problem with the discrepancy that exists between youth justice and child welfare policies is that there is an implicit assumption that children in need of care and protection, and children in need of control, are two distinct groups. Clearly this is not the case at all, particularly for children and young people in the care system who may enter care on the basis that they are in need of care and/or control. Under the Children Act, these individuals are simply children in need, who are therefore vulnerable. The contradiction is that once a child commits a criminal offence, the fact of their vulnerability may be swept under the carpet. Yet, at the same time as developing some tough youth justice provisions, the government has demonstrated a commitment to improving the life chances of children and young people in care.

Reducing offending

In 2001 a new project on reducing offending amongst looked-after children was added to the list of projects in the Quality Protects programme. This was seen by some as an important indication that the government was beginning to pay attention to the link between care and offending. The project team began by developing the following target: by 2004 the proportion of children aged 10–17 and looked after continuously for at least a year, who have received a final warning or conviction, should be reduced by one third from the September 2000 position. This sets a target to reduce the proportion from 10.8 per cent to 7.2 per cent (DH 2003a).

In light of the tough line that has been taken by the government with children who do get into trouble, it is questionable how far this target can actually be achieved in practice. However, the very existence of the target should at least encourage local authorities to focus on *how* they might reduce offending rates. After developing the new target, the project team commissioned the National Association for the Care and Resettlement of Offenders (NACRO) to undertake research to determine good practice in reducing offending by looked-after children.

One of the key points emphasised in the resulting good practice guide (NACRO 2003b) is the need for a strong link between social services departments and youth offending teams. This is regarded as vital if there is to be an effective response to the offending of looked-after children. Effective information sharing is seen as a critical part of this endeavour. As I have argued elsewhere, in order to achieve justice for looked-after children, those involved in sentence planning must be made aware of their vulnerability and their 'care' status (Taylor 2003). It is also important to ensure that looked-after children do not become lost in the criminal justice system.

Another pertinent issue raised in the good practice guide concerns the offending of young people in children's homes. The situation described is certainly a cause for concern.

> There is much anecdotal evidence to suggest that young people in children's homes are more likely to be prosecuted for relatively minor offences, such as damage to property, carried out within the home. If these young people had been living in their own families, it is likely that this behaviour would be dealt with in a very different way. (NACRO 2003b, p.16)

In order to address this problem, some local authorities have implemented protocols between Social Services and the police, setting out guidelines for residential staff on how best to respond to disruptive behaviour. As NACRO (2003b, p.17) observes, such protocols certainly have the potential to reduce the unnecessary criminalisation of children in residential care. Indeed, they may be an important way forward in terms of trying to meet the target on offending rates outlined above.

Whilst the existence of a reducing offending project team is important in itself, it is generally accepted that it has not had a particularly high profile in the overall Quality Protects programme. This is perhaps because the government's policies on protecting vulnerable children and preventing criminality do not sit comfortably together. With this in mind, it is interesting to consider current government proposals for an 'intensive fostering' service to be developed with respect to persistent young offenders. This would involve offenders being placed with specially trained foster parents.

A recent White Paper on antisocial behaviour (Home Office 2003c) outlines the government's plans to develop intensive fostering as an alternative to custody. It is thought that intensive fostering will be aimed particularly at 10- and 11-year-old offenders who consistently commit low-level offences but cannot be locked up unless they commit very serious crimes (cf. Travis 2002). Therefore, although intensive fostering is being presented as an 'alternative' to custody, in actual fact it may be more accurate to view it as a disposal that 'enables' the removal from home of very young offenders.

Whilst remand fostering services have existed for some time, intensive fostering is arguably a conceptually different type of disposal that could potentially criminalise increasing numbers of very young offenders. On a more general level, it is also likely to increase the association in the public mind between the care system and criminality. How the development of an intensive fostering service fits in relation to programmes such as Choice Protects also needs to be considered, as carers are already a very scarce resource. Having said this, a recent evaluation of a specialist fostering scheme in Scotland (Walker, Hill and Triseliotis 2002), offering placements to young people who would otherwise be in secure residential accommodation, highlighted that young people could benefit from such schemes. '[E]ach young person in the study was thought to have benefited from being in the scheme, with overall outcomes rated as "good" for over a third' (2002, p.222). It remains to be seen whether intensive fostering will have a similar impact.

Child welfare and youth justice: Joined-up or disjointed policy?

This chapter began by outlining the government's wider social exclusion agenda and the emphasis on the need for joined-up policy. Early intervention programmes such as Sure Start and universal services for adolescents such as Connexions both have the potential to provide valuable support to families and individuals who may be at risk of social exclusion. More specifically for young people in care, the Quality Protects programme and the subsequent development of the Children (Leaving Care) Act 2000 represent key steps forward in improving the life chances of looked-after children and care-leavers.

A key strategy adopted by the government is their 'rights and responsibilities' approach. Yet, in relation to young offenders, this strategy appears to have become skewed in one direction. Children and young people are increasingly required to take responsibility for their actions, which is important. However, their rights as children under the

UN Convention on the Rights of the Child may be easily overlooked by certain provisions in the Crime and Disorder Act (Goldson and Peters 2000) and by prison service policy (Utting 1997).

Whilst more positive aspects of youth justice are those that emphasise offender reintegration and restorative justice, it is important that the implications of such measures are thought through. Even the seemingly less punitive referral order, which allows offenders to make amends to victims and/or the wider community, may have harsh consequences for young people. For example, the fact that an individual can be referred to a youth offender panel on his or her first offence could have a net-widening effect. Bringing more young people to the attention of the justice system at an early age opens up the possibility that they will be dealt with more harshly at a later date (cf. Thorpe *et al.* 1980).

Increasing numbers of young people have been placed in custody in recent years (Home Office 2003a), despite the fact that the links between disadvantage and offending are well documented. A recent review of the evidence (Smith 2003) reveals that young people entering the criminal justice system in 2000 were at greater risk of a custodial sentence than they were a decade ago, and the sentences they received were on average longer; although this may have had more to do with punitive sentencing in the adult courts than in the youth courts (Smith 2003).

The problem is not only that incarceration is stigmatising for young people and can lead to future social isolation and exclusion, but also that many individuals will re-offend after release (O'Neill 2001). Many of the more punitive measures in current youth justice legislation have the potential to seriously undermine the government's wider concern with tackling social exclusion. In this sense, New Labour's approach is far less joined-up than we are led to believe. Whilst early intervention initiatives, such as Sure Start, may offer valuable support to pre-school children from disadvantaged areas, the punitive nature of certain youth justice provisions may well end up stigmatising and socially excluding these exact same children as they get older.

On a more hopeful note, there are some signs that the government is keen to 'join up' services for vulnerable children. Recent proposals for new Children's Trusts (DfES 2003d) would involve bringing together local services for children in need, including health, education and social services, but also potentially youth offending teams. It is arguable that youth offending teams should be seen as essential rather than potential partners in this new organisational structure.

Furthermore, one way in which current trends in youth custody may be reversed is through the greater use of community-based sentences. Current government proposals include rolling out ISSPs as the main response to serious and persistent offending (Home Office 2003b). Recent research has shown that ISSPs can engage young offenders in purposeful activity, in ways in which short, disruptive spells in custody cannot (see Youth Justice Board 2003b). It is essential that such alternatives to custody are now promoted as serious options for those involved in sentencing.

Conclusion

The New Labour government has introduced a wealth of new legislation, programmes and initiatives since 1997, making for a very dynamic policy climate. Various positive new measures concerning the welfare and protection of vulnerable children have been developed, yet interestingly these have been far less publicised than the series of youth justice policies introduced. Few people seem to have heard of Quality Protects, yet the government's 'tough on crime' agenda is well known.

Why should youth justice policies be better publicised? Being seen to be 'tough on crime' is certainly regarded as an election-winner (although justifications for 'get tough' policies often serve to fuel what Garland (2001) describes as the 'crime complex' of late modernity, whereby a heightened fear of crime becomes commonplace regardless of national crime rates). Perhaps an equally important explanation for the fact that Quality Protects and related initiatives are little known is that the public are largely indifferent to the situation of children and young people in care (Colton 2002).

This chapter has explored New Labour's two-pronged approach to youth policy – promoting the welfare and protection of vulnerable children and preventing criminality. It has been argued that this approach has resulted in the development of some incoherent and contradictory policies, which are likely to have a disproportionate impact upon young people in the care system. In particular, there has been a discrepancy between the government's stated objective of reducing the number of children locked up and recent trends in the use of youth custody. There has also been a failure to place the welfare of children at the heart of the youth justice system, despite national and international condemnation of the way we treat children in trouble.

So what are the implications of the current climate for young people in care who break the law? In brief, attempts to reduce the offending rates of looked-after children may be seriously undermined by more punitive approaches to dealing with children in trouble. Given that young people who have been in care are three times more likely than their peers to receive a caution or conviction (DH 2001a) and are over-represented in the prison population, it seems reasonable to assume that current youth justice measures will have a disproportionate impact upon them. Yet harsh responses to children in trouble are rarely helpful (e.g. Lipsey 1995) and do not sit comfortably with the government's commitment to improving the life chances of vulnerable young people in care.

Promoting alternatives to custody and trying to join up services for vulnerable children are two ways in which we could move towards reconciling some of the tensions in current policy. There are some indications that both of these approaches are beginning to be officially encouraged in certain quarters. As for our understanding of the link between care and crime, it is crucial that reducing offending by looked-after children becomes a much more prominent part of the life chances agenda in the future.

Chapter 3

Introducing the research study: Theory and method

Introduction

One of the central aims of this study is to question the generally accepted relationship between care and criminal careers. With this in mind, this chapter explores how theoretical insights from criminology can usefully inform research on foster and residential care. To date, criminological theory and child-care literature have tended to exist in two separate intellectual and professional domains, and there have been few attempts at integration. Through the central construct of 'attachment', this chapter seeks to make some connections between the two areas of study. Both have drawn on ideas about attachment, but interpreted and used these ideas in quite different ways.

After advancing a theoretical framework to inform the research, the chapter moves on to outline the methods adopted in relation to the empirical work upon which subsequent chapters are based. A case is made for using qualitative interviews in research on a sensitive topic and there is a discussion of sample selection, data collection and analysis. There is also a brief presentation of the demographic profile of the young people interviewed for the research.

Attachment in criminology

In his social control theory of delinquency, Hirschi (1969) sees the delinquent as a person relatively free of the intimate attachments, aspirations and moral beliefs that bind most people to a life within the law. A person is free to commit delinquent acts because his or her ties to the conventional order have somehow been weakened or have failed to form. In considering why individuals conform, Hirschi points to the influence of the social bond. When the social bond and parent–child attachment are strong, he states that it is less likely that the child will engage in delinquent behaviour. Hirschi identifies four elements of the social bond, which may be glossed as follows:

- *Attachment* emphasises sensitivity to the opinion of others; as Hirschi explains, 'If a person does not care about the wishes and expectations of other people…he is to that extent not bound by the norms. He is free to deviate' (p.18).

- *Commitment*: The extent to which an individual is committed to conventional lines of behaviour determines how much he or she has to lose. For example, an individual who is committed to a particular career is likely to avoid actions that may jeopardise his or her career prospects.

- *Involvement*: The more an individual is involved or engrossed in conventional activities, the less time he or she will have to indulge in crime.

- *Belief*: People vary in the extent to which they believe they should obey societal rules, and 'the less a person believes he should obey the rules, the more likely he is to violate them' (p.26).

Attachment to parents is one of the key variables in control theory. Hirschi's data indicate that the more attached a child is to his or her parents, the lower the risk of delinquency in that child. However, it is questionable how far such intimate bonds can be established in the context of care.

Attachment in care

Bowlby, Fry and Ainsworth (1965) claimed that 'foster homes cannot provide children with the security and affection that they need; for the child they always have a makeshift quality' (p.137). They noted that children are not slates from which the past can be wiped clean, but are human beings who carry their previous experiences with them. Their behaviour in the present is deeply affected by what has happened in the past. Whilst emphasising the 'baggage of disadvantage' that many young people bring with them into care, Bowlby *et al.* also emphasised the importance of attachment. They argued that it is unlikely that an intimate bond will develop in the context of care unless a child is placed with carers before the age of two. However, this view paints a very black-and-white picture of attachment, suggesting that it either develops at an early age or not at all. This is a notion that has been much criticised in later work (see e.g. Tizard 1986).

In contrast to Bowlby *et al.*'s (1965) claim, the interview data in this study (see Chapters 4–7) indicate that it is possible for attachments to develop with a substitute care-giver even when the relationship begins well after early childhood. This finding is supported by Schofield *et al.*'s (2000) recent research (see also Schofield 2003). Whilst such attachments may not be as intimate as the biological mother–child bond, they are nevertheless still very important and meaningful in the lives of young care-leavers. It therefore seems that we need to distinguish between different levels of attachment when talking about the importance of the concept, rather than regarding it as unidimensional. Admittedly, more recent work in the area of attachment has gone some way to addressing this issue (Ainsworth *et al.* 1978; Main 1991), and Bowlby himself developed and refined his own ideas right up until his death in 1990.

Whilst it is certainly possible for quality attachments to develop in the context of care, the appropriate care conditions clearly need to be in place in order for this to occur. Conditions such as placement stability and security are, however, notoriously difficult to achieve for many young people. Indeed, the high incidence of movement in care has already been documented in Chapter 1, as have the potentially disruptive consequences for young people who frequently change placements.

Attachment as a central construct

Further consideration of the issue of attachment has the potential to inform our understanding of the care experience and can perhaps go some way towards explaining why a disproportionate number of young people who have been in care will go on to offend. Attachment is a theme of central importance in two distinct intellectual and professional domains, child care and criminology, and is arguably the key construct in attempting to bridge the literature in these areas. However, the mechanisms and processes behind attachment are not the same in the two areas of study, and an important task is to tease out the differences.

Hayslett-McCall and Bernard argue that Hirschi's (1969) version of attachment contrasts strongly with that provided by Bowlby (1969).

> Hirschi describes the absence of attachment as natural (i.e. the Hobbesian state) and asserts that people enter into bonds of attachment only as a result of socialisation. In contrast, developmental psychologists describe attachment as a natural inborn need and assert that the unattached state (detachment) arises only when there is a traumatic failure of the environment to meet that natural need. (Hayslett-McCall and Bernard 2002, p.6)

In the child-care and social work literature, individuals who are securely attached in quality relationships tend to be regarded as stable, confident, socially able individuals, whose relationships are reflected in the quality of their social life. By contrast, individuals who are involved in disturbed, hostile, unstable or insecure relationships are more likely to experience pain and unhappiness. As Howe (1995) points out:

> children raised in emotionally fraught families can become angry, confused and difficult. Women in relationships with impulsive, insecure and jealous men may find themselves the victims of violence. And those who feel unsupported and unloved can feel lonely and distressed. (p.1)

Such individuals frequently become the social worker's concern.

In the world of the child-care professional, issues surrounding attachment are often discussed in conjunction with psychological definitions and therapeutic interventions. For example, the attachment classification system developed by psychologist Ainsworth and colleagues (1978) distinguishes between different types of attachment such as secure, insecure-avoidant and insecure-ambivalent. Secure attachment is the preferred type, whereby a parent's care is consistently responsive and the child clearly prefers his or her mother or care-giver over strangers. Insecure-avoidant attachment is evident when children show few apparent signs of distress at separation, and ignore or avoid the parent when he or she returns. Finally, the insecure-ambivalent type becomes highly distressed when separated from his or her parents, but remains very difficult to calm down when they return.

More recent work in this area (e.g. Main 1991) has added the concept of disorganised attachment. Meanwhile, disorders of non-attachment have also been identified in some extreme cases in which children have never had the chance to form affectionate bonds with other people. Whilst it is questionable how far we can place human beings, who are inherently complex creatures, into such neat categories, such a classification system does at least offer a multi-dimensional understanding of attachment.

Howe (1995) outlines three broad social work responses to difficulties with the attachment process: understanding, support and psychotherapy. Strong links are often made with maternal deprivation theory (Bowlby 1951) and more recent developments in the discipline of psychology. The (in)ability to form secure attachments to a care-giver tends to be related to previous family experiences and, traditionally, social workers have focused on damage limitation for the 'unattached' child who comes into their care.

Attachment (or lack of it) is interpreted, and responded to, slightly differently in the domain of criminology. Whilst theorists increasingly regard early family experiences as a highly significant factor in explaining people's ability to form pro-social attachments (e.g. Hirschi 1969; Sampson and Laub 1993), there is generally less importance attributed to psychological health and the therapeutic. Rather, a primary concern, of social control theory at least, has been whether or not an individual is sufficiently bonded to his or her family and society to deter him or her from involvement in crime. Attachments are regarded as important by criminologists because they can deflect individuals from a criminal career trajectory, or prevent delinquent behaviour from being initiated in the first place.

Relational theories of crime

One of the particularly useful ideas in Hirschi's (1969) theory is that the formation of valued attachments in a network of relationships should be protective against offending. Yet, interestingly, Hirschi's later work with colleague Michael Gottfredson (Gottfredson and Hirschi 1990) abandons this relational emphasis (Taylor 2001). Gottfredson and Hirschi (1990) contend that low self-control is the individual-level attribute that causes crime at all ages, when combined with appropriate opportunities and attractive targets. They suggest that whilst self-control differs between individuals, it tends to remain constant over time within a given person and is generally set by about the age of eight.

Gottfredson and Hirschi's discussion of self-control as a time-stable individual trait completely neglects the impact of external, structural factors on individuals in later life, thereby conflicting with Hirschi's earlier work. Whilst the self-control theory also abandons the emphasis on relationships that is evident in Hirschi's earlier theory of social control, a relational emphasis has been picked up more recently in the work of other criminologists.

Braithwaite's (1989) general theory of crime control suggests that the key to crime control is cultural commitments to reintegrative shaming. Braithwaite distinguishes between reintegrative shaming and stigmatisation. He suggests that stigmatisation occurs when shame is applied injudiciously and counterproductively, the consequence of which is likely to be attraction to criminal subcultures. This is because deviant subcultures can supply the outcast offender with an opportunity to reject his or her rejectors. By contrast, reintegrative shaming means that expressions of community disapproval will be followed by gestures of re-acceptance.

According to Braithwaite, the best place to see reintegrative shaming at work is in loving families: 'family life teaches us that shaming and punishment are possible while maintaining bonds of respect' (p.56). Braithwaite goes on to state that parents should punish in a consistent manner, which is within the context of love, respect, and acceptance of the child. He claims that 'individuals are more susceptible to shaming when they are enmeshed in multiple relationships of interdependency; societies shame more effectively when they are communitarian' (p.14). It is noteworthy that Braithwaite's emphasis on interdependency is taken directly from traditional control theory (Hirschi 1969).

In trying to explain crime across the life-course, Sampson and Laub (1993) have combined Braithwaite's theory of reintegrative shaming (1989) with elements of control theory to produce a unified model of informal family social control. The model focuses on the three dimensions of discipline, supervision and attachment. According to Sampson and Laub, the key to all three components 'lies in the extent to which they facilitate linking the child to the family and ultimately society through emotional bonds of attachment and direct yet socially integrative forms of control, monitoring and punishment' (p.68). Their theory is consistent with the view that social bonds to family and school can inhibit delinquency in childhood and adolescence (Braithwaite 1989; Hirschi 1969). Sampson and Laub also suggest that there is continuity in antisocial and deviant behaviour throughout life and across various dimensions, such as crime and alcohol abuse (cf. Gottfredson and Hirschi

1990). However, they note that despite these continuities, attachments formed in later life – to the labour force and marriage – can sharply mitigate criminal activities.

The life-course perspective

This section focuses on the life-course approach from a criminological perspective (although there is also a life-course approach within child welfare, which has its roots in developmental psychology – see for example Parkes, Stevenson-Hinde and Marris 1991).

The life-course perspective emphasises stability *and* change over time.

> In other words, while the long-term view embodied by the life-course focus on trajectories implies a connection between childhood events and experiences in adulthood (continuity), the simultaneous shorter-term view implies that transitions or turning points can modify (change) the course of life trajectories – they can 'redirect paths'. (Sampson and Laub 1995, p.144)

With regard to the element of continuity, Laub and Sampson (1994) found that 'the same childhood antisocial behaviours are predictive of educational, economic, employment, and family status up to eighteen years later' (p.248). Whilst certain commentators view stability of behaviour patterns as biologically and/or psychologically determined (e.g. Wilson and Herrnstein 1985), Laub and Sampson suggest that social variables such as the family offer more important insights.

In relation to the element of change, Sampson and Laub (1996) question what the potential escape routes are that may overcome childhood misbehaviour. In their re-analysis of the Gluecks (1950) data, they found that military service during World War II offered American men from economically disadvantaged backgrounds an opportunity to better their lives through on-the-job training and further education. According to the authors, 'G.I. Bill training in the transition to young adulthood predicted occupational attainment and socio-economic well-being at age 32, especially among former delinquents' (1996, p.364). Whilst GI Bill training was not a protective influence in itself, it did enable individuals to get into education and training and thus enhanced the opportunities available to them.

More recently, Laub, Nagin and Sampson (1998) have reiterated the importance of good marriages in the desistance process. They found that 'early marriages characterised by social cohesiveness led to a growing preventative effect' (p.237). Laub *et al.* suggest that entering the social institution of marriage provides the potential for informal social control on some high-rate offenders. They conclude that 'of course, our perspective suggests that outcomes are always in doubt, but that is even more reason not to give up hope based on negative returns from the early years alone' (p.237). This last statement has important implications for any theoretical framework that aims to inform research on care.

In spite of the 'baggage of disadvantage' that many children and young people bring with them into the care system, we should not simply regard the role of care as 'damage limitation'. Rather we should seek to consider how care might be made a more positive experience, and which factors in the care experience might protect against the risk of subsequent offending behaviour. The life-course perspective in criminology offers a particularly valuable relational approach with which to think through such issues.

Sampson and Laub (1993) note that attachments formed in later life to societal institutions, such as family, school and work, can sharply mitigate criminal activity. Their criminological theory illustrates that attachment is not only significant at the individual and structural level, but also at different points throughout life. This understanding of attachment offers a contrast to much of the child-care literature that has traditionally applied attachment theory exclusively to very young children and studies of development in the early years (although there are increasingly exceptions to this, e.g. Downes 1992; Schofield 2003).

Using the notion of attachment in relation to both individual and structural factors also implies that there are different levels in terms of the degree of attachments made. In other words, the quality of attachment may vary depending on to what or whom you are actually attached. This removes any temptation to regard the concept in relation to a simple securely attached–non-attached dichotomy. Interestingly, criminology has had less to say about the different degrees of attachment made, in terms of the quality of social relationships. For example, Hirschi's (1969) definition of attachment implies that you are either sensitive to the opinion of others or you are not. Neither has criminology seriously considered the mechanisms and processes behind attachment, and this is an area where it could benefit from engaging with the child-care and psychology literature.

A consistent finding throughout the literature is that, even with prolonged early negative experiences, there is a very marked heterogeneity of outcome amongst young people (Rutter *et al.* 1998). So what are the mechanisms involved that enable certain individuals to be resilient in the face of previous psychosocial adversity?

Vulnerability and resilience

Rutter *et al.* (1998) note that 'broken homes' have been featured as a risk factor for antisocial behaviour since the beginning of criminological research in the last century. Various studies have demonstrated that individuals who have been in care have an increased likelihood of being delinquent (Minty and Ashcroft 1987). Some children who have experienced most of their rearing in residential group care have a particularly high rate of antisocial behaviour (Quinton and Rutter 1988). However, even with prolonged severely negative experiences, there is enormous variation amongst children in their responses.

According to Rutter *et al.* (1998), several main themes have emerged in the resilience research in relation to protective and risk factors. Potentially protective factors include a lack of genetic vulnerability, a high IQ, a warm and secure relationship with at least one parent, good parental supervision, good experiences at school and a prosocial peer group. Rutter *et al.* further note that these protective processes may involve a broad set of underlying mechanisms, although they admit that their research has certainly not led to any firm conclusions. Of their eight listed mechanisms, the following seem to be particularly relevant to young people in care:

- reduction of negative chain reaction (e.g. avoidance of negative coping strategies such as drug/alcohol use)

- promotion of self-esteem and self-worth (such as through secure and supportive relationships)

- opening up of positive opportunities (as through educational/career opportunities)

- positive cognition processing of negative experiences (acceptance rather than denial or distortion).

Rutter *et al.* (1998) conclude that life experiences continue to be important in the course of a criminal career after childhood: 'Pre-existing dispositions and later experiences will work on each other in a cyclical and cumulative way, but people can also break out of patterns as a result of beneficial turning points' (p.380). There is no reason why the care system could not seek to offer beneficial turning points for children and young people who are looked after, whilst promoting the four protective mechanisms listed above.

In fact, Howe *et al.* (1999) have recently explored those four mechanisms further, and considered them specifically in relation to children who are dealt with by social workers. The formation of secure and supportive relationships is arguably one of the key factors. Many people measure the quality of their social life in terms of the quality of their social relationships (Howe *et al.* 1999) and often it is the knowledge that people care about us that enables us to care about ourselves. When we care about ourselves our feelings of self-worth are likely to increase, and we may be less likely to adopt negative coping strategies.

Interestingly, the concept of resilience is becoming increasingly popular amongst social work researchers and practitioners. Robbie Gilligan's (2001) work in this area demonstrates that the concept of resilience can usefully inform social work practice. In *Promoting Resilience* Gilligan notes that 'the main message of this book is one of hope: that the lives of children in the care system can be made better, even by little things, and that what we – social workers and carers do – can make a difference' (2001, p.1). As Gilligan goes on to point out, the idea of resilience 'runs counter to a well-embedded tradition in helping and caring services that looks first for the deficits, the pathology, the problem' (p.1).

Gilligan's work reflects exactly the kind of attitude towards young people in care that I want to emphasise in this chapter. Increasing recognition of the importance of resilience in the social work field is a very positive step in the right direction to improving young people's experiences of care. It is noteworthy that Schofield (2001) points to the conceptual overlap between resilience and attachment theory. 'The conceptual overlap should make practitioners feel comfortable about using both frameworks and both terminologies, since they are entirely compatible' (p.11).

Research that emphasises offenders' capacity for change is also useful in the context of the current study. Maruna's recent work on desistance (2001) is particularly valuable in this sense. His research calls into question the 'myth of the bogeyman', whereby social deviants are regarded as fundamentally different from the rest of us. Maruna's in-depth interviews with both active and reforming offenders convincingly demonstrate that ex-offenders can turn their lives around for the better. As Maruna points out, the proliferation of self-help groups and literature in modern society indicates that many of us believe that that we can change our own lives and behaviours. However, we do not always extend this belief in the ability to change to other people.

A theoretical framework for research on care

A theoretical framework for research on care, and specifically research on the link between care and crime, could usefully be based on a life-course perspective that emphasises the interplay between stability and change throughout life. In relation to crime, this perspective illustrates that experiences in later life can sharply mitigate criminal activity (Sampson and Laub 1993). A further condition for the theoretical framework is that it should be relational, emphasising the importance of being strongly embedded in a network of relationships with law-abiding others (Braithwaite 1989; Hirschi 1969). The driving force for this relational life-course perspective is the concept of attachment – a theme of central importance in both child care and criminology.

Whilst child care and social work have traditionally regarded attachment as a psychological variable, it is arguable that we need to move beyond an individual-level understanding of attachment. Developments in criminology offer us the opportunity to do so. At the same time, there are useful lessons to be learnt from child welfare in terms of the mechanisms and processes behind attachment. Both areas of study have drawn on ideas about attachment, but interpreted and used these ideas in different ways. The discussion has highlighted the potential value of bringing together the two literatures.

In addition, there are also productive links that could be made between research on resilience in child welfare and research on desistance in criminology. The former emphasises individuals' capacity to overcome previous disadvantage, the latter focuses on the capacity to move beyond past criminal behaviour. Whilst taking account of what has occurred in the past, both approaches are concerned with the potential of individuals to lead positive, productive lives in the future.

A sophisticated theoretical framework on care needs to consider the complicated interplay between continuity and change in young people's lives, with particular reference to the conditions that enable different levels of attachment to develop. At the most basic level, young people must experience placement safety and stability during their time in care. Without these fundamental conditions in place, the development of quality relationships is very difficult to achieve. Although the care system does not always provide the appropriate conditions for attachments to develop in the first place, we should look to the cases where young people *do* develop secure attachments in care, considering the factors which may have enabled them to do so (e.g. Schofield 2003).

Theoretical insights from criminology, which emphasise pathways and turning points throughout life, offer a useful wider frame of reference in which to think more positively about the potential of those in the care system. Indeed, child-care professionals should regard themselves as active agents in helping to determine young people's futures. An emphasis on futures plural indicates that there are a variety of pathways that individuals may take through life, and that outcomes in adulthood are not necessarily set in stone. As Quinton and Rutter (1988) note, 'clearly, the potential for change remains for a long time; notions that it is "too late to do any good" are rarely justified' (p.222). An important task for carers, social workers and policy-makers alike must surely be to promote this attitude throughout the system. The recent interest in resilience in the family placement field (e.g. Gilligan 2001) is certainly compatible with this view.

Having introduced the theoretical framework that informs my work, this chapter will now focus on how the research was conducted in practice, focusing particularly on the methods used and issues of data collection and analysis.

Research questions and background

The research in this book came about as a result of my interest in the care system, which originally stemmed from my own experience of being in foster care as a teenager. As a 'looked-after' young person I became quickly aware of the largely negative perceptions of care that existed amongst the general public. Since I was fortunate enough to have had a very positive placement, other people's perceptions did not match the reality of my own experience. My interest in the taken-for-granted assumptions about the care system and the young people within it then developed further during my time as a criminology student at Lancaster.

In broad terms, the research aimed to question the taken-for-granted relationship between experiences of care and criminal careers. A further aim was to give a voice to young people who had been in care, with a view to learning from their experiences. More specifically, I was concerned with the following questions:

- What aspects of the care experience might promote social inclusion and help to reduce the disproportionate number of care-leavers who become part of the young prisoner population?

- What are the mechanisms involved that enable certain individuals to be resilient in the face of previous psychosocial adversity?

- How might developments in modern criminological thought inform social work practice and provide a wider theoretical framework for research on local authority care?

The third question has been largely dealt with above. However, some of the key theoretical concepts are discussed further in later chapters in relation to empirical findings. With regard to the empirical work, I was particularly interested in gaining first-hand accounts and experiences from individuals who had been through the care system. It is for this reason that qualitative interviews were conducted with those who had actually been in care. The research was exploratory in nature, aiming to illuminate aspects of the care experience that might be significant in protecting against offending behaviour. Rather than developing or testing a particular hypothesis, the intention was to explore the diversity of care careers, allowing young people to tell their own stories of how the care experience had affected their lives.

Of course it is important to bear in mind that the data produced from this kind of exploratory approach will be based on subjective accounts that it is not possible to validate elsewhere. Schofield (2003, p.14) has identified several different kinds of data that can result from retrospective interviews with adults who have been in care. This includes what actually happened, what people remember happening and what people have been told or remember having been told happened. The memories of care-leavers may be further complicated by the often traumatic of their earlier experiences and by the fragmented picture that they may have as a result of movement and change. However, at the same time, and as Schofield's (2003) own interviews with adults who grew up in foster care demonstrate, retrospective interviews with care-leavers can generate extremely powerful insights.

Using qualitative interviews in research on a sensitive topic

In order to illuminate aspects of the care experience that may be protective against offending behaviour, a decision was made to explore the experiences of both care-leavers who were in custody and care-leavers who were not. The choice to interview those in custody inevitably meant that I would be speaking to one extreme of the population who have been in care. Part of the original rationale behind this was that it might enable some comparisons with those who had avoided custody and who were not known offenders although, in fact, it turned out that not all who were interviewed outside custody had managed to avoid custody or criminal behaviour during their life. Given the qualitative focus of the research, this was not a major problem as the main task was still to explore the diversity of individual pathways through care.

In light of the time and resources available, qualitative interviews with young people who had been in care seemed to be the most appropriate method in terms of the research aims. As Emler and Reicher (1995) state: 'if one wishes to understand the significance of delinquency – or indeed of any activity – in the lived experiences of adolescents, then one must start from the evidence of that experience' (p.xiii).

The term 'qualitative interviewing' generally refers to in-depth, semi-structured or loosely structured interviews, what Burgess calls 'conversations with a purpose' (1984, p.102). Such interviews are particularly useful in exploring experiences that could not be adequately described in closed-ended questions. As Mason notes, a more unstructured interviewing approach 'lays emphasis on depth, complexity and roundedness in data, rather than the kind of broad surveys of surface patterns which, for example, questionnaires might provide' (1996, p.41). In addition, such an approach places importance on the narrative provided by the interviewees, allowing them more freedom and control to articulate their experiences.

Qualitative interviews also allow for flexibility, enabling the researcher to modify questions, avoid some and consider what is appropriate in the context of specific interview situations. This is particularly important in research on a sensitive topic, and research on care experiences is nearly always sensitive as the vast majority of young people who enter care do so in difficult circumstances. Research into sensitive areas can of course threaten those being studied because of the level of emotional stress that it produces (Lee and Renzetti 1993). This was something of which I was acutely aware during my research, and I did my best to ensure that the interview experience did not give rise to unnecessary distress. As the British Society of Criminology's code of ethical practice (2003) outlines, researchers should strive to protect the rights of those they study, their interests, sensitivities and privacy.

Issues of confidentiality and anonymity were addressed at the beginning of each interview, where it was also made clear that participants would only be required to discuss issues with which they felt comfortable. All research participants were assured that there would be no records of the interview with their name on and that all names would be changed in the dissemination of research results. Interviewees were asked if they were happy for their interview to be recorded and assured that I would be the only person who listened to the tape or mini-disc recording.

In terms of interview style, I began with a fairly unstructured approach, homing in on more specific issues as the interview progressed. After introducing myself and the research, and addressing the serious issues of confidentiality, an attempt was made to put the young person at ease. Tony Parker's classic opening line, 'What did you have for breakfast this morning?' (see Soothill 1999, p.238), brought a smile (or at least a curious look) to several of my respondents' faces. Following this, the young people were asked to tell me about their story of being in care, from when they first went into care to when they left. This very unstructured question allowed them to describe their experiences in their own words. Some individuals responded really well to this type of questioning and spoke at length about their life in care. Others were less open and gave only the minimum of detail, gradually opening up in response to more specific questions.

As the interview continued, more structured questions were introduced as I tried to build on what the respondent had already said. Yet often many of my own specific concerns had already been answered when the respondents told their 'story', such as the number of placements and type of placements that they had experienced. Howeve in case some of the key details of an individual care history had not been addressed, interviewees were asked to fill out a very basic one-page questionnaire at the end of the interview. This asked for some basic quantitative facts, such as age, age on entry to care, number of placements and so on. Such data were obviously helpful in terms of understanding individual pathways through care, but the questionnaire also served as a consistency check on what had previously been said.

Key themes that I was interested in exploring during the interviews included care history, family relationships, relationships with carers and social workers, school and education, and after-care experiences. Where it had not already arisen, the issue of criminal behaviour was introduced following questions on the level of control in care and whether or not it was considered easy to break the rules in different placements.

It is noteworthy that I found insights from feminist thinking very useful in planning the research. As Reinharz (1992) states, 'feminist researchers generally consider personal experiences to be a valuable asset' (p.258) as they can not only increase empathy with research participants in certain cases but also repair a project's pseudo-objectivity. In other words, by acknowledging the importance of their own personal experiences, feminist researchers can highlight that traditional positivist claims to scientific objectivity are not always as objective as we are led to believe. On a similar note, Stanley and Wise (1993) argue that the researcher is an active presence, an agent in research whose own self and experience cannot be left behind.

Having been a looked-after young person myself, I was able to draw on various personal contacts in my search for willing interviewees. The existence of these contacts inevitably influenced the research design.

Interview sample

The majority of interviews were conducted between September 1999 and October 2000, and at the end of this time I had spoken with a total of 39 young people who had been in care. Interviewees were accessed from a range of locations in the north-west and south-east of England. Ten young men were interviewed in a young offender institution and ten young women were interviewed in a women's prison. These particular individuals were identified with the help of prison and probation officers. The remainder of the sample (n=19) was accessed through various leaving-care schemes and through the use of a 'snowball' sampling strategy. This latter approach involved me enlisting the help of personal contacts, such as foster carers and care-leavers, and asking for them to suggest anyone whom they knew who might be willing to take part in an interview.

Table 3.1 Age distribution of young people by gender

	Male	Female
16–17	2	9
18–19	10	11
20–27	3	4

Table 3.2 Age at first entry to care by gender

	Male	Female
Under 5	1	1
5–9	4	5
10–14	9	9
15–18	1	9

Table 3.3 Experience of foster and/or residential care by gender

	Male	Female
Just foster care	1	7
Just residential care	6	3
Both	8	14

Fifteen of the interviewees were male and 24 were female. They ranged between 16 and 27 years of age, with the most common age being 18 for both males and females (see Table 3.1). Amongst those interviewed in custody, there was nobody older than 20.

Whilst there was a wide range of ages at which individuals first entered the care system, the most common age at first entry to care was 15 for females and 14 for males (see Table 3.2).

Interviewees in this study described a very diverse range of care experiences. However, more than half had experienced both foster and residential care provision (see Table 3.3).

One striking point about the profile of the young people in this study is that far more females than males were accessed for interview. The question of why this should be so is an interesting one that has important implications for the way that the data are analysed and interpreted. Those interviewed in prison custody (n=20) were divided equally between males and females. However, amongst those outside custody, I found many more young women than young men who were willing to take part in an interview. It is quite possible that my own gender had an impact here, and it may also be the case that females tend to be more comfortable sharing sensitive and personal experiences. An additional explanatory factor may have been my own age. I was 23 during the majority of interviews and quite close in age to many of those with whom I spoke. The fact that I was not older may have discouraged some potential interviewees from coming forward (although equally it could have encouraged others).

As I have commented elsewhere (Taylor 2003), it is also important to note that, to some extent, the experiences and responses of young men and women would be different due to varied expectations, pressures and stereotypes. Similarly, overall recorded offending rates for men and women are vastly different. Females offending rates are never as high as male rates in the first place, and females tend to 'grow out' of crime more quickly. The peak age of offending in 2002 was 19 for males (having been 18 since 1988) and 15 for females (Home Office 2003d). Such issues are important to bear in mind when considering young people's stories.

Of this largely self-selecting interview sample, just one individual was of mixed race origin and just one was registered as disabled. Some of the specific experiences that these individuals described were undoubtedly interesting in their own right. However, in presenting the interview data in the space available, I have chosen to focus predominantly on issues that relate to as many of the young people as possible. Consequently issues of race and disability are not addressed in the chapters that follow.

Data analysis

All the interviews that were recorded in this study were transcribed, and then analysed along with written notes using the Atlas t/i computer-assisted data analysis package. As well as enabling a range of different analyses, this package served as a data management tool. One particular technique adopted in order to increase the validity of the findings was deviant-case analysis (cf. Silverman 2000). This involved actively seeking out deviant cases or negative instances in the data. The discovery of deviant cases can encourage researchers to continually modify their argument until it has the best degree of fit with the data produced.

One of the potential problems for qualitative researchers who use small samples is how far they can generalise from their research results (cf. Oakley 1999). My position is that it is possible to generalise from a small number of cases if the theoretical concepts used to understand the cases are shown to be illuminating. As Pawson and Tilley (1997) note, the process of generalisation is essentially one of abstraction: 'we move from one case to another, not because they are descriptively similar, but because we have ideas that can encompass them both' (p.119). They further suggest that it is sets of ideas and theoretical notions that are transferable between cases, not lumps of data.

Distinguishing between statistical and logical inferences, Mitchell (1983) makes a similar point. According to Mitchell,

> the extent to which generalisation may be made from case studies depends upon the adequacy of the underlying theory and the whole corpus of related knowledge of which the case is analysed rather than on the particular instance itself [sic]. (p.203)

He further suggests that in the social sciences an illuminating case can make new theoretical connections apparent. The important point being made is that it is not the typicality or the representativeness of the case itself that allows us to generalise from it, but the cogency of the theoretical reasoning. A useful example in which to illustrate this is Goffman's classic study *Asylums* (1961). The concept of a 'total institution' was developed in his study of just one asylum, but has been adopted widely in the social sciences as theoretically illuminating.

One way in which I attempted to increase the generalisability of my findings was by combining qualitative data extracts with quantitative measures of populations. This approach, advocated by Silverman (2001), also helps to avoid the problem of 'anecdotalism' in qualitative research, whereby only a few exemplary instances of particular experiences are provided in project reports. In presenting the data I attempted to use simple counts where possible in order to give a sense of how far a particular experience was representative of the entire sample. In addition, particular findings in this study were compared to quantitative findings from other research.

Conclusion

In summary, this chapter began by introducing the key theoretical concepts used to inform the research, focusing particularly on the central construct of attachment. It has been argued that theoretical insights from criminology, which emphasise pathways and turning points throughout life, offer a useful wider frame of reference in which to think more positively about the potential of those in care. Such insights are entirely compatible with the recent interest in resilience in the family placement field.

Following the theoretical discussion, there has been an outline of the methodological approach adopted for this study, which involved using qualitative interviews to explore individual pathways through care. A primary aim of the research was to illuminate aspects of the care experience that might be protective against offending behaviour. In trying to understand the relationship between care and criminal careers, I spoke with both care-leavers in custody and care-leavers outside custody. Their experiences are described in the following four chapters.

Part II
Young People's Experiences

Chapter 4

Exploring the residential care experience

Introduction

Plagued by constant scandals of abuse in recent decades, the residential care sector continues to suffer from being seen as 'a last-resort measure for children separated from their families' (Corby, Doig and Roberts 2001, p.35). Children's homes are strongly associated in the public mind with delinquency (Warner 1992), and it has been suggested that those 'dumped in public sector oubliettes' (Hansard 2003, col. 554) may emerge as fundamentally different from the rest of 'us'. Such negative stereotypes abound and inevitably impact upon the young people who live their lives in residential care. Although these are often some of the most difficult children in the care system (Davies *et al.* 1998), they nevertheless deserve exactly the same chances, opportunities and quality of care as all other children. The development of new National Minimum Standards for children's homes (DH 2002a) will, one hopes, go some way to improving their situation.

However, minimum standards alone cannot break down negative stereotypes and raise aspirations. This requires broader attitudinal change. With this in mind, this chapter uses the voices of young people to explore various aspects of life in residential care, highlighting that the taken-for-granted link between residential care and crime is not always as straightforward as is commonly assumed. In order to understand why residential child care is often 'a recurrent theme in offending behaviour' (Stewart *et al.* 1994, p.83), it is important to try to appreciate something of the residential experience as it is lived by young people. This is the aim of the current chapter.

Of the 39 young people interviewed in this study, 31 had experienced a placement in residential care (which included all 20 of those who were interviewed in custody). These placements were generally in mainstream children's homes, but included boarding schools, secure accommodation, remand centres and a residential college for physically disabled people. Three interviewees who had been in residential care were placed with siblings at a very young age prior to long-term foster placements. Just nine young people had only ever been in residential care, whilst most had experienced a combination of both foster and residential placements.

A placement breakdown in foster care frequently resulted in a young person's admission to a children's home. However, one individual actively chose not to enter foster care in the first place, commenting that given the 'harsh situations' he had known in his life, the idea of a foster family was completely alien to him. Whilst these feelings were not the norm amongst the young people interviewed, they do indicate the continuing need for residential child-care provision (Utting 1997). In spite of the criticisms that are made of the residential sector, children's homes remain an essential service for some.

Feelings on entry to care

Regardless of what type of placement young people enter, going into care can be a very difficult experience in itself. Whether entry into care is a crisis intervention or a planned event, memories of what it felt like often stay with individuals for a very long time. Even those who are relieved about escaping an abusive situation at home may fear the prospect of going somewhere new and leaving behind all that is familiar. It is arguable that residential care may initially be more overwhelming and intimidating than foster care, because new residents have to contend with meeting different children and staff, rather than just a single family.

Greg (18) recalled his first placement at age 11, which was in a children's home: 'When I first went in there I was shaking all over.' Liz (17) went into care when she was aged six, with her siblings:

> I was a bit excited really, something different, until I realised what was actually happening. I got a bit upset like. [*pause*] She didn't, me mum and dad didn't come and see me... I didn't really realise what it was all about, I thought they were gonna come back.

The emotions young people recalled on entering residential care ranged from scared, angry and depressed to excited and relieved. One thing they did all have in common was vulnerability. Of the 31 young people who had been in residential care, just seven reported that they had experienced a placement that they enjoyed. Interestingly, three individuals stated that their positive experiences were in small children's homes with about four or five residents. These three had all had negative previous experiences in larger children's homes and were of the opinion that smaller units were most definitely preferable. The main reason given was that fewer residents means more attention and one-to-one contact with staff for the individual – an issue that will be picked up on later.

For others, such as Gail (17), their low expectations of the care system meant that they were pleasantly surprised by the reality of their situation.

> When I went into care it wasn't as bad as what I thought it was gonna be. I thought it was gonna be like people telling you what to do, but it wasn't like that. It was people trying to understand, you know, that you've got problems and that, and trying to help you deal with them. It was quite good really.

It is important to note that positive experiences of life in residential care did exist amongst the interviewees. Unfortunately, such experiences were few and far between when compared to the stories of misery and mayhem that emerged.

Mayhem in residential care

Twenty-three young people spoke of getting into trouble, becoming involved in offending behaviour or absconding during their stay in a residential setting. 'Kids running wild' was a common phrase used by several individuals when telling their stories of life in residential care. The picture that emerges from many of these stories is one of complete mayhem. It is of course important to note that 11 of these 23 individuals said that they had been in trouble with the police for criminal offences prior to their admission to care. Yet whilst some young people came to residential care with a history of offending, others began offending only after admission. The stories told by young people are undoubtedly a serious cause for concern.

The police were there everyday, it was ridiculous...we had a six-year-old little girl running around with plastic knives and forks trying to stab people. Kids getting up on the roof, setting the fire alarm off, just totally destructive. (Beth, aged 19)

We'd all climb out in the middle of the night and run wild. We'd all sniff gas in the back garden or get pissed and come back effing and blinding. We'd get done for breach of the peace. Stupid things really. (Gemma, aged 18)

Even the girls were pinching cars and smashing windows of the kids' home. And running riot and pinching money out the office and all kinds of stuff. (Michael, aged 18)

I were in a kids' home...and I were out pinching and that. I were doing heroin and I were always running off and that, absconding. And then I'd come back, have a shower, get a change of clothes and then I'd be off again. You know, claim me pocket money and that. (Dave, aged 19)

Given that 23 out of 31 young people who had been in residential care described similar experiences to those outlined above, it seems very important to consider which aspects of the residential care experience may facilitate, or indeed protect against, offending behaviour. How do individuals become involved in crime and delinquency during their time in a residential setting, and what reasons do they themselves give for their own behaviour? In line with the research methods used for this project, all the details of individual care histories that follow are obtained from young people.

Involvement in crime

Young people's own stories indicate that there may be several different reasons for becoming involved in crime whilst living in residential care. Mixing with deviant others and not having anyone who cares emerge as significant themes in the following tales.

Mark (19) was serving his third custodial sentence at the time of interview. He went into care when he was aged 13 because his father was unable to cope with him. Mark's father had got custody of him and his siblings the previous year, and after moving from his mother's house Mark claimed to have gone 'off the rails'. He was staying out late and getting drunk with his friends; they used to get picked up by the police in the early hours of the morning and brought home. Mark had one caution before going into care.

> Claire: Did you get into any trouble at all when you were in the children's homes?
>
> Mark: That's when I started getting into trouble with the police. I had no one to tie me down then, no one telling me what to do really, so I was just going out doing what I wanted. When I was at home I was worried about what me dad would say if I got into trouble with the police and that. But when I got placed into care, I had no one to worry about then... At the start of it, there was a lad there who I started knocking about with. I started knocking about with the people that he knocked about with, and we ended up getting into cars, shoplifting, stuff like that...as soon as I was placed into care I thought that 'Well no one cares', so I just went out and done me own thing then.

It is not possible to say whether Mark's progression from antisocial behaviour to criminal offences would have occurred had he stayed at home and not gone into care. However, the story he tells is a recurring one in this study and particularly familiar amongst the group of young men who were interviewed in a young offender institution. The vast majority of these young males were involved in varying degrees of anti-social behaviour prior to admission to care, but reported that their behaviour had sharply escalated towards crime and delinquency once in the care system.

Mark did not say a great deal about the other boys he was mixing with when he went into the children's home, but the implication is that he began to hang around with those who were already involved in crime. However, of particular interest is his point about feeling that he had nobody to worry about once he went into care and, in turn, nobody was worried about him. The feeling that nobody cared about them once they were in care was a point made by several other young people.

Donnie (19) had been in and out of jail since he was 17. He went into care when he was aged 14. He has dyslexia and had been expelled from two schools because he was having problems and causing trouble. His parents did not know what to do with him and so he was placed in a children's home. He had two cautions before going into care.

Donnie: Basically I got all my criminal convictions from when I was in care and from when I've left care... When I went into care, you went in and you had to like be with the high people...people who were like Top Dogs or whatever. And we were basically just pissed out of our heads, coming back whatever time we wanted to come back... I was just going out and getting in trouble with everyone else, getting in trouble with assault charges, theft charges, burglary charges and all kinds of stuff... I just went straight downhill.

Claire: Yeah, why do you think that was?

Donnie: I don't know really. Errm me head must've been thinking like me mum and dad didn't want me, but they did, they just couldn't cope with me. But I just thought, well if nobody cares about me, then I shouldn't care about myself.

It is interesting to note that, like Mark, Donnie describes his entry into care as something of a turning point in terms of his behaviour, commenting that he went 'straight downhill'. In addition, the idea that nobody cares is put forward again.

The feeling that nobody cared was made particularly explicit by Gemma (18). She had been in care since the age of three because of abuse at home, and at the time of interview was in the young offenders' unit where she had been since she was 16. In her opinion being in prison custody was preferable to being in care.

I'd rather be in here than in a kids' home...because here you know that you've got someone watching out for you 24 hours a day, *there* people just don't give a shit what you're doing. That's the reason why I run wild, because nobody gives a fuck.

The Who Cares? Trust's survey of over 2000 children in care in the UK (Shaw 1998) asked young people: what is the best thing about being in care? The most frequently occurring response to this question was 'having someone who cares', which was mentioned by 21 per cent of all respondents. However, this was only mentioned by 12 per cent of young people in residential homes and 11 per cent of young people in residential homes said 'nothing' was the best thing about being in care (Shaw 1998, pp.56–7).

Clearly, having someone who cares is very important to most of us, as it makes us feel worthwhile and that we are worth caring about. Furthermore, we know that quality attachments to law-abiding others can protect against offending behaviour (Hirschi 1969). However, attachments to carers in residential homes are often particularly difficult to develop, as the survey results above and stories such as Gemma's suggest.

Peer pressure and the need to fit in

When explaining how they began getting into trouble in residential care, several young people raised the issue of peer pressure from other residents (often older boys), as well as their own desire to fit in.

John (18) had been in and out of jail four times since he was 15. He went into care at the age of seven when his mother was sent to prison. He did not meet his father until he was 16. At first John was placed in foster care, but when he was 12 he began getting into trouble and shoplifting. At 14 he was placed in a children's home and says this is when his involvement in crime stepped up a level, as he began mixing with the older residents. He said:

> It used to hold up to 16-, 17-year-olds, and I was like knocking about with all of them… I used to go out with them and pinch cars, I was easily led when I was in that place, I'd have done anything.

As for John's view of children's homes:

> There's crime there, that's all there is. And you know when 15-year-olds get sent to the local authority for pinching a packet of sweets, I feel sorry for them 'cos them are going in them. And they'll go back to court for burglary charges or something because of the children's home. It's got them like that 'cos of the people that's in there.

John offers a combination of factors in explaining his own behaviour. On an individual level he notes that he was 'easily led' and would have done anything. However, he also highlights the difficulties of moving into a home with older residents who were involved in crime and delinquency. This latter point was made in a different way by several other young people, who emphasised the great importance of fitting in.

Greg (18) first went into care when he was aged 11: his parents had split up. He says he ended up 'having a temper' and his mum was unable to cope with him. Greg started committing crimes with other children from the residential home where he lived when he was 13. He had his own clear view of why so many other residents did likewise.

> When they go in care they've got to fit in haven't they, they've got to join in with everyone else…if someone says to them 'D'you wanna go out and do something?' they're gonna say 'Yes' 'cos they wanna fit in.

exclusion

Fitting in was, not surprisingly, seen as particularly important by those who had been subject to some of the most serious peer pressure in the form of bullying. Being bullied emerged as an important theme in the interviews and as something that clearly stays with young people for a very long time afterwards. It is worth noting that bullying was not an issue that I specifically asked about during the interviews, yet five young people spoke of being bullied during their time in residential care.

Neil (19) did not go into detail, apart from noting why he had 'hated' living in children's homes: 'I kept getting bullied every time I was there you see.' Liam, however, went into quite specific detail about his experiences and how they had affected his subsequent behaviour. Liam (26) went into care when he was aged 12. His parents had both died and he was living with his grandmother, but she was unable to cope with him as he was constantly fighting and getting into trouble at school.

Describing his initial experiences in the children's home where he was placed, Liam commented: 'I was getting fairly regularly beaten up when I first went in…just by older boys in there…that was for about three months.' Later he talks about getting into trouble at school when he was still living with his grandmother. He says he was very angry about the death of his parents and wanted someone to blame:

> You know I was just fighting or nicking stuff, drinking. I mean I was getting absolutely drunk when I was 12, so living at home with my gran, she couldn't take it… When I went into care it sort of stepped up a level. There was a lot of peer pressure and that. You know you might not want to do something, but if everyone's there you've got two choices, get in trouble with the people you live with or get in trouble with staff. And if you're living with people you've got to get on with them, so it's an easier life going out and getting arrested, because then you're all right in their eyes, you know, they trust you… I mean there was stuff I wasn't really wanting to do… I knew it was wrong, I *do* know right from wrong, I *did* do at that age. But it was just an easier life… Went out on two burglaries and really did not enjoy that at all, it

was a really uncomfortable, nasty feeling, but if I didn't do it, you know, I would have got beaten up and stuff.

Liam had not been in trouble with the police prior to his admission to care. However, by the time he left care he had been charged with various offences including car theft, burglary and arson.

> Claire: So you reckon like once you go into care it's fairly easy to…?
>
> Liam: …Yeah a lot easier to get arrested than not, a lot easier. And there's so much pressure on you to, you've got to get on with the people who live there 'cos you're living there 24 hours a day. I mean staff, you get staff that help, you get staff that don't help, but staff that help are only there like certain days a week. There's no one there constant…the only people who are there constant are the people who are living there, so that's who you've got to get on with.

Towards the end of the interview I asked Liam what the worst thing about being in care was.

> I suppose the bullying really, just getting beaten up at two o'clock in the morning and nothing I could do about it…it went on for about three months. Then…I started getting in there, into trouble and stuff… And then they sort of left me alone, thought I was all right. So if I hadn't of got into trouble then I would have continually got a beating, and you know when there's like four or five of them just laying into you, punching and kicking…

In their study of 48 children's homes, Sinclair and Gibbs (1998) found that 44 per cent of children they talked to had been bullied during their stay and 14 per cent had been taken advantage of sexually. Liam's account provides us with some idea of the effect that bullying can have on young people's subsequent behaviour. It also gives a sense of the power of peer pressure in residential care. As far as Liam was concerned he had two choices: getting in trouble with the people he lived with or getting in trouble with the staff. He convincingly demonstrates why he felt the latter was preferable.

Universities of crime

Regardless of whether young people claim to have been bullied or pressured by their peers, or whether they equate their offending with not having anyone who cares, the one constant theme through virtually all of the scripts above is that a delinquent subculture always already exists when individuals enter residential care. In other words, there is always a crowd to follow. Stewart *et al.* (1994) found in their study that residential care was frequently 'a ready made community within which crime was condoned by the subculture of delinquent peers on hand day and night to reinforce social norms' (p.84). Many of the stories told here support this finding, and suggest that a 'university of crime' concept may be applicable to certain residential care units, particularly in explaining how residents pick up criminal 'skills' regardless of whether they have previously been in trouble or not.

According to Michael (18): 'If I hadn't been in care I wouldn't know half the things I know now…like how to pinch a car or something basic like that. Or how to take an alarm off a shop or whatever.' Meanwhile, Gemma (18), who went into care when she was three, felt very strongly that she would not have ended up in prison if it were not for being in care nearly all of her life.

> Because I wouldn't be mixing with the environment what I was mixing with in care…going out robbing people, taking drugs and that, sniffing gas and that. I didn't have a clue about any of that until the kids' homes. People showed me things like that and I didn't have a clue.

According to Polsky (1962), institutionalised adolescents are probably more socialised by their peers than any other group in society. Certainly this may explain the experiences described above and how young people picked up a criminal record whilst involved in deviant activities *away* from the home. Interestingly, other young people picked up a criminal record specifically through their behaviour *inside* the residential home where they lived. Their stories draw attention to the routine prosecution of minor offences in some children's homes. Many local authorities have had a policy of reporting to the police any children who cause criminal damage and assault staff in their units. Whilst such policies exist to protect staff and the general home environment, in some cases they seem to have resulted in the unnecessary criminalisation of looked-after children (cf. NACRO 2003b).

For example, two young females reported having left their respective children's homes with criminal records because of assaults on staff. Both suggest that the staff may have been a little over-zealous in their reactions.

Tracy (16) had never been in trouble with the police before going into care at 15, yet she left residential care with two assault charges on her record. She describes one assault on a member of staff, which resulted in her receiving a fine.

> I was messing about in the kitchen…and I wouldn't get down off the side, I was looking for something… And I just got down and I was like in a hyper mood and I pushed the door to get out the way and it just hit her on the shoulder…she took me to court.

It is arguable that birth parents would be highly unlikely to respond to such behaviour by taking their child to court.

Donna (16) was particularly bitter about the assault charges she had received.

> My criminal record is through care, for assaulting staff. I've got nowt else on my record apart from one charge…if I'd have flicked me fingers and it accidentally caught them it was assault, do you know what I mean?

Although we only have the young people's interpretation of events here, their stories illuminate yet another aspect of the residential care experience. They also highlight the serious need to consider what actually constitutes 'assault' and 'criminal damage' in local authority homes. In recent research commissioned by the Department of Health, NACRO (2003b) also identified this problem, commenting that the threshold for calling the police in a children's home can be low. As mentioned earlier (p.52), some local authorities are now beginning to address this issue by implementing protocols between Social Services and the police, setting out guidelines for residential staff on how best to respond to disruptive behaviour (see NACRO 2003b). The intention is to encourage staff to question when it is actually appropriate to respond to an incident by calling the police. Such protocols may prove crucial in preventing young people from entering the criminal justice system at an early age simply because they are in the care of the state.

Letting off steam

A further reason for offending in residential care that I wish to explore falls under the broad heading of 'letting off steam', which relates to serious past trauma affecting current behaviour. We know that the majority of children and young people in care today have experienced some degree of stress in their lives, and an increasing number enter the system specifically because of abuse or neglect (DH 2003b). Whether subject to sexual assault, regular beatings and/or the unpredictability of alcoholic and drug-abusing parents, for many children (and not just those in care), these experiences become the norm. Or to put it another way, this is life as they know it.

Being removed from an abusive or stressful environment (such as when an admission to care takes place) may enable some young people to get back to being a child again. However, it is often only at this time that the impact of people's previous experiences actually begin to hit them. Consider the stories of the following three young people. They all potentially fall into the letting-off-steam category (although there may be other reasons for their offending as well).

Adele (19) was serving her second custodial sentence at the time of interview. She went into care when she was 13 after running away from home because of having 'problems' with her father. Adele did not explain what these problems were, other than to say that she was scared of her father. She notes that she had never been in any trouble at all before going into care.

Adele: No, never, I was a little goody.

Claire: What do you think changed?

Adele: It was just being away from home and knowing that I didn't have me dad watching me all the time… I wasn't scared of me dad [*because she was away from him*] and just wanted a taste of freedom.

Andrea (16) was also in prison when I interviewed her. She was placed in care by Social Services when she was 13 because of physical abuse by her father, who was an alcoholic and had psychiatric problems. Up until going into care Andrea says she had been trying to look after herself and her father but found she was unable to cope. She had never been in any trouble before entering care.

> When I was with me dad, I had never been in trouble with the police in me whole life. I goes into care and this happens, I just went off the rails… My temper just went out of control, I just lost it.

Andrea went on to note that she enjoyed living in the children's home and was made to feel welcome by both staff and residents: 'But living with other children with the same problems is hard.'

Like Adele and Andrea, Beth (19) had never been in any trouble with the police before going into care at 15. Her mother was an alcoholic who had a succession of boyfriends and Beth often ended up getting abused by them, either physically or sexually. She went to Social Services and asked to be put into care. After being placed in a children's home, Beth began drinking heavily, used drugs and received charges for criminal damage, assault, shoplifting and being drunk and disorderly. She had been to court, fined, bound over and had spent time in police cells, but she had not been to prison. She says of care:

> It was a lot better than the situation I was in in the first place. But I think I made things worse for myself… I don't know how much to put down to the fact that I was in care, and how much to put down to the fact that I was, I suppose disturbed, I was a teenager! …I was at the stage where I thought, you know, they're smashing milk bottles up, I just fancy doing that. I think I did a lot of things because I could do them.

Beth also remarked on the difficulty of living with other children with problems (cf. Berridge and Brodie 1998), thus echoing Andrea's comments.

> You couldn't go to bed thinking 'Oh I'll get up in the morning, have breakfast with so-and-so, it'll be a really nice day.' You were like waiting for the next bad thing to happen, waiting for the next police van to come round the corner, waiting for the next kid to do a bunk 'cos their mum's fucked off again. You were taking on board everyone else's problems at the same time as your own, which you couldn't help but do 'cos you were living with them.

None of these girls had ever been involved in any trouble at all prior to entering care, yet all left the care system with criminal records. Both Andrea and Beth had experienced abuse at home. We may speculate that Adele had also experienced abuse, but we cannot be certain as she did not choose to elaborate on her home situation. Adele noted that she began getting into trouble because she was away from home and wanted some freedom. Andrea, on the other hand, stated that she just lost it, whilst Beth spoke of becoming involved in offending simply because she could. On the basis that all three had moved from difficult home circumstances, it is possible to regard their behaviour in residential care as letting off steam or letting go of some anxiety and emotion.

It may be significant that the three individuals above were all young women. Several other individuals in the study also spoke about letting go of some anxiety and emotion, but in the form of self-harming. This was not a topic that I actually asked interviewees about, but seven young people volunteered the information that they had self-harmed and/or felt suicidal during their time in care. All seven were female, and there may be more than one reason for this. It is possible that the young women found it easier to disclose such sensitive information to another female; equally, females in general may be more comfortable discussing their feelings and emotions.

Another possibility is that women are more likely to harm themselves than men are. Indeed, prison research highlights that there is a greater incidence of self-harming and suicide amongst female inmates (Howard League for Penal Reform 2001). What the experiences of some individuals in my study suggest is that residential care staff, like prison officers, must know to look out for the signs of self-harming amongst young people. Unfortunately, getting to know young people and their behaviour can be very difficult when staff are constantly coming and going.

Staff continuity

Having someone who cares is one factor that can potentially protect individuals from becoming involved in crime. However, developing quality attachments to carers in a residential setting tends to be very difficult to achieve. Indeed, one of the important issues that several young people touched on was that of staff continuity in residential care. Seven individuals specifically outlined how difficult it is to get to know staff, and indeed care about what they think, when so many staff are coming and going all the time. All noted that this constant movement contributed to a general lack of stability in the homes.

> The people that run the actual children's home, they were always swapping over, so we never got a chance to speak to anyone about anything, or if we did, they wouldn't be there any more. The next

person who came along wasn't clued up enough to know what was happening in our lives. (Jackie, aged 18)

I would like to say one thing now, the children's homes aren't as homely as foster care, the children's homes have people coming and going, and they move on... The staff, it's like you get used to one, then they do an overnight shift and then they move on. And then another one comes along, and then a couple of weeks later they could just be like gone forever and you don't know. (Tracy, aged 16)

Beth (19), meanwhile, expressed the view that staff did not actually care about the residents anyway.

Claire: So you felt that the staff at the home were there just because they were being paid?

Beth: Well they'd say it... 'Go out and get pissed, I don't care. I'm getting paid to watch you.' [*laughs*] That was it. It wasn't 'Well is there anything else you can do instead, are you feeling that bad?' I mean...at the end of the day I know it's a wage coming in, I know that, but we're people, you can't just leave people... Like when there's staff coming and going, they get paid a wage for doing this and they've got all their shifts set, and they swap their shifts round. I don't know, they don't make any attempts to disguise the fact that they are just doing it for the money. That's what makes it bad you know, they're not actually here because they give a shit, they're here because they're getting paid four quid odd an hour to look after us.

Clearly, it is difficult to get to know staff when they are constantly coming and going in the homes. Where there is a lack of staff continuity, it seems inevitable that there will also be a lack of stability and security for the residents. Furthermore, if young people have difficulties getting to know staff, they may feel unable to open up about any problems that they are experiencing, such as being bullied. As Beth suggests, a simple thing like being indiscreet over swapping shifts can be picked up on by young people, and may serve to reinforce their existing belief that nobody really cares.

In spite of the stories above, however, it should be noted that it is not impossible to form attachments to carers in a residential setting. Five young people in this study did talk of being close to a member of staff (and several others spoke more generally about staff being helpful).

Anne (18) simply stated that: 'I very much got fond of some of the staff and had a good relationship with some.' Neil (19), on the other hand, spoke of one specific lady who had worked in two of the children's homes where he stayed, but who had actually died after a couple of years. 'She was the only friend I ever had in the children's homes… I still think of her to this day.'

Similarly, Billy (16) was also able to name one specific member of staff whom he had got close to in residential care and who still sent him Christmas cards and presents despite the fact that he had left the home where she worked some time ago. Whilst it is good to see that it is possible for young people to form close relationships with carers in a residential home, this was unfortunately not the norm amongst the majority of individuals in this study. Few people felt that they had someone they could really talk to. Of course, when young people do not care about the feelings of the staff, and feel that they themselves are not cared about, they are far less likely to be bothered about rules and sanctions in the home.

Rules and sanctions

Nearly every young person who spoke of getting into trouble whilst in residential care noted that it was very easy to do so, although the reasons for thinking this were quite different. Few felt that the staff had the power to impose sanctions that would have any significant effect on young people. Perhaps this is one reason why the police may be more likely to become involved with incidents than elsewhere (NACRO 2003b).

Greg (18) noted that not many children in one of the homes where he lived ever went to school (an issue that will be picked up in Chapter 6), but felt that the staff did not really care anyway.

> They weren't bothered if you know what I mean… They just said if you're not going to school don't stay in all day, go out and do something. They would ask you to leave the children's home until school time was properly over, you're not there then are you.

Kate (25) described how she and another girl used to regularly abscond, running away to London for a few days at a time: 'Being grounded meant nothing. The police would be notified that we had disappeared, but they would just be waiting outside the home for our return. A joke really, why bother?' Meanwhile, Michael (18) explains how the staff reacted to him being in trouble all the time:

> Like I'd get arrested for something, get kept in and go to court in the morning, and then they'd bail me back to the local authority. And then I'd go back to the kids' home and they'd take me ice-skating. And then I'd come back, have tea, they'd give me some money, so I'd go out for the night, do something else, get in trouble with the police, come back and they'd take me go-carting or something. I don't know, it was just, they just weren't arsed. They just wasn't bothered, and I was trying to grow up dead fast.

Kate questions why the staff even bothered grounding her and her friend, as it 'meant nothing', whereas Greg and Michael interpreted the staff's lack of reaction to their respective behaviours as a sign that they could not care less. One could argue on the basis of these stories that residential staff are, in some senses, damned if they do and damned if they don't. If they impose a sanction such as grounding a young person, it gets ignored anyway. However, if they accept as given the young person's behaviour then they appear not to care.

The difficult situation faced by staff in residential care (cf. Whitaker, Archer and Hicks 1998) was in fact recognised and acknowledged by some individuals. Joe (18), for example, questioned why children would listen to staff when they had not listened to their own parents trying to control them. Dave (19) had a similar view: 'There's not much they can do, but they do try.'

There was a general consensus amongst the young people that there is very little that staff can do to control unruly residents, who are themselves usually well aware of this fact. Having said this, John (18) pointed out that sanctions that involved preventing residents from going on activities were frustrating: 'Some of the rules are easy to break but some of them aren't, 'cos you used to go to Flamingo Land and stuff. But if you'd done something wrong you wouldn't go. So you'd lose really.'

Activities and involvement

The activities available in some residential homes certainly seemed to be considered one of the more positive aspects of being in care. In fact, when asked what the best thing about their care experience was, five young people (who were all male) referred to the activities that they had been involved in. For example, Ian (17) mentioned: 'You get to go swimming every other night or so.' And Liam (26) said that 'There was always something happening…going to the cinema or swimming, mountain bikes. I mean I wouldn't have had that at home.'

Kane (19) noted that during the three years he had spent in a residential care placement, he went abroad four times doing a range of outdoor pursuits, such as snowboarding and mountaineering. According to him, 'I've done everything.' Four of the girls also mentioned that they had enjoyed some of the activities and days out that they had been on. Yet, interestingly, whilst emphasising the fact that they too would not have been to so many places had they not been in care, Gail and Liz were not quite so certain that this was such a good thing.

Liz (17) felt that all the good things about care only served to reinforce the feeling that her situation was not a normal one: 'You get spoilt, you go out on day trips, you get everything you want…it's not like being in a normal family though.' Meanwhile, Gail (17) remembers being taken to McDonald's and Alton Towers by social workers when she was younger, and then going home and moaning at her mother because she could not afford to do the same: 'They're giving you a life that nobody else, not many people, can live up to in a way.' She goes on to suggest that day trips and activities in care ought to be reduced a little. The issue of over-compensation for young people in care is a difficult one, particularly given that so many of these individuals may just crave a 'normal' life. As Gail indicates, spoiling young people in care can also create tensions if and when they return home. Having said that, activities can provide a very important focal point for those in long-term residential care who have little else to look forward to.

It is perhaps possible to make a distinction between the effect of one-off or short-term activities and engagement in long-term pursuits. The latter is arguably more likely to encourage young people to develop interests and a commitment to a particular hobby. It also opens up the possibility that individuals will see progression in their own abilities, which can in turn contribute to an increase in self-esteem.

Unfortunately, this distinction is not relevant to the children's home where Beth lived, as there was very little opportunity to go out at all. This is because the residents were regarded as too badly behaved and there were not enough staff to supervise them. Beth therefore felt that her situation was fairly bleak: 'You're not encouraged to move on when you're in a home, you just exist, that's it. You're still breathing, you've been fed, you've got clothes on your back, that's it. There's nothing extra.' Hirschi (1969) suggests that the more an individual is involved or engrossed in conventional activities, the less time he or she will have to indulge in crime. On a related note, boredom was identified as a cause of deviant behaviour by some individuals. For example, Adele (19) commented: 'We just wanted to go on a bit of a mad one because we'd been bored.' However, for those who were able to go out doing activities whilst in care, it is worth noting that, regardless of whether they enjoyed them or not, involvement in activities did not appear to protect against offending behaviour. There was just one exception.

Ben (18) went into care when he was aged eight, and says he had been shoplifting the year before that. At the time of interview he was serving his sixth custodial sentence. Although Ben seems to have been in trouble with the police from a very early age, the intriguing thing about his story is that he claims he was rarely in trouble in the children's homes. He used to abscond most weekends to go home to be with his friends: 'Nearly every time I'd go home at the weekend I'd get arrested.' Yet, according to him, he always had activities to keep him occupied when he was in care during the week and therefore never felt the need to get into trouble: he was 'too busy going swimming and stuff like that'.

Ben was the only person in this study whose involvement in activities apparently protected him from getting into trouble (cf. Hirschi 1969). For the majority of young people though, activities did not appear to have any significant impact on their offending behaviour. This is perhaps because activities can presumably only take up so much of young people's spare time. A worrying finding in this study was that several young people often had a great deal of time on their hands in the day because they were in-between schools or simply not attending school. The education of young people in care is an issue that is explored in Chapter 6. However, I want to consider now one specific way in which the residential care experience could be improved.

Improving the residential care experience

Having smaller units in residential care was a theme that emerged on several occasions in this study. Recall that three out of the seven young people who claimed to have enjoyed a placement in residential care stated that these placements were in smaller units with about four or five residents. All had had negative experiences in larger children's homes. Jackie (18) described how she and her sister stopped going out at night and getting into trouble when they moved to a smaller home with just five residents: 'It was more like a family…loving, you know…you get more done for yourself, do you know what I mean? Instead of done in a group it's more about you.' It does seem to follow that if there are smaller units, then each young person is likely to receive more individual care and attention. Fewer residents may also mean fewer staff and if there is only a small number of staff then the residents may have more opportunity to get to know them. A smaller staff group may also contribute to staff continuity, thereby providing more stability and routine for the young people (and potentially opening up opportunities for long-term residents to develop attachments).

Furthermore, smaller units may help to avoid the behavioural problems that can occur when large groups of young people live together (Frost *et al.* 1999). Young people who have been in residential care certainly seem only too aware of how residents can influence each other.

When asked how he thought the care system could be improved, Joe (18) offered the following response:

> Well the children's home I was in, there was about four or five of us criminals in there. I reckon if they try and spread 'em about a bit more so there weren't so many criminals in the same building.

Apparently thinking along similar lines, Liam (26) emphasised the need for smaller units.

> I know it would cost money to have a smaller unit, but there wouldn't be the pressure there… If you've got 15 kids and one's sort of bullying everyone else into doing stuff, that one kid is affecting 15 people's lives. So, you know, if you've only got four or five there, there's less chance. I mean most people in care are in care because of reasons like loss of family, being uncontrollable and stuff, but you do get the ones who are proper wrong-doers. If they had smaller units there's less chance of them having one of those there, there's less chance of everyone sort of snowballing.

The stories told by some of the young people in this study certainly support the view that residential care experiences may be improved when units are smaller. This is also an issue that has also been emphasised in recent literature (Davies *et al.* 1998; Frost *et al.* 1999; Sinclair and Gibbs 1998). According to Frost *et al.* (1999), 'the effectiveness of residential care units is enhanced when they are small, perhaps providing around 6 places' (p.124). In fact, the average capacity per children's home in England has been falling in recent years. The last available statistics from the Department of Health show that, at 31 March 2000, 50 per cent of homes accommodated six or fewer children, compared with 43 per cent in 1997 and 37 per cent in 1995 (DH 2001b).

However, it is noteworthy that whilst only a small percentage (9 per cent) of the total number of homes in 2000 accommodated 13 or more children, this actually worked out as being 101 homes (DH 2001b). A small number of these homes held over 21 residents. In light of the evidence provided in the stories above, and also the wider calls for smaller units (e.g. Frost *et al.* 1999), it seems that the government ought to be making a concerted effort to reduce the capacity of as many of their larger units as is possible. In spite of the criticisms that are made of the residential sector, children's homes remain an essential service for some individuals. It is therefore crucial that a sustained effort is directed towards making young people's residential care experience as positive and productive as possible.

Summary

This chapter has explored the residential care experience by using the voices of young people to illuminate various aspects of life in residential care, with particular reference to offending behaviour. The majority of young people who had been in residential care (23 out of 31) spoke of being involved in offending during their stay and various reasons for this were put forward. One significant theme to emerge was not having anyone who cares. Several individuals commented that because they felt that nobody was worried about them, they in turn had nobody to worry about, and were therefore free to behave as they wished. It is important to note that 11 young people in the current study claimed to have been in trouble with the police before being admitted to care, but 23 spoke of being in trouble with the police once in care.

In the postscript to his report on the abuse of children in care in Gwynedd and Clwyd, Sir Ronald Waterhouse (2000) remarked that the care homes had been notably unsuccessful in terms of crime prevention. Amongst those giving oral evidence to the tribunal, it emerged that 52 complainants had convictions prior to entering care, but 85 were convicted of offences whilst in care and 85 received convictions after leaving care. Waterhouse concluded that 'some children who had not offended before were introduced to delinquency and to harsh regimes in which they were treated by some staff as "little criminals"…some regimes *encouraged absconsion and increased offending*' (2000, p.840, emphasis added).

The stories and experiences that have been presented in this chapter support Waterhouse's claim that individuals may be introduced to delinquency in children's homes. Certain aspects of the residential care experience can promote delinquency in some cases and increase offending in others (cf. Cornish and Clarke 1975). In understanding why residential care is a recurrent theme in offending behaviour, there is clearly a variety of factors at play – ranging from local authority policies on the prosecution of minor offences in children's homes, to bullying and peer pressure by other residents. If the quality of care provided in the residential sector, and our aspirations for young people within it, are ever to be raised, then such issues need to be seriously addressed. Only then can we hope to reduce the number of individuals who continue to leave residential care with a criminal record. In the following chapter I focus on more positive experiences of care, exploring further the importance of having someone who cares.

Chapter 5

Developing secure attachments in the context of care

Introduction

Objective One of the government's objectives for children's social services is 'to ensure that children are securely attached to carers capable of providing safe and effective care for the duration of childhood' (DH 1999). This relates to the wider concern of providing placement stability and security for young people in the care system, something that is notoriously difficult to achieve. In the year ending 31 March 2002, 15 per cent of looked-after children experienced three or more placements. In the same year, of those foster placements that finished, just 9 per cent had lasted for two years or more and 2 per cent for five years or more (DH 2003b).

As research by Sinclair, Gibbs and Wilson (2000) highlights, long stays by children in the same foster home are comparatively rare. Foster placements themselves are not in great abundance either as local authorities frequently have difficulty in recruiting and retaining sufficient carers. The shortage of placements inevitably means that placement choice for children and young people tends to be a luxury – despite official assertions that 'choice protects' (see DH 2002d). Given that so many young people are not actually 'matched' with their carers, the likelihood of attachments developing is often rather haphazard. In addition, many young people will carry a 'baggage of disadvantage' with them to their placements. Experience of previously abusive relationships at home, for instance, can leave individuals feeling vulnerable and fearful about forming new relationships with adults.

Drawing upon Hirschi's (1969) broad definition of attachment, which emphasises sensitivity to the opinion of others, this chapter explores how far it is possible to develop quality prosocial attachments in the context of care. In particular, can older children develop attachment relationships with their carers? If so, how might these relationships impact upon a young person's own identity and self-image, and can they help to protect against involvement in crime?

The foster care experience

This chapter focuses particularly on young people's experiences of foster care because the few close relationships formed by interviewees in residential care were mentioned in the previous chapter. There was also a discussion of the difficulties of forming relationships with staff in children's homes, particularly when there is a lack of staff continuity. It is generally accepted that foster care tends to provide a more realistic opportunity for young people to develop attachments to their carers. This was certainly the case in the current study. In addition, the levels of attachment to carers that were reported by some individuals appeared to be on a far deeper level in foster care than they were in residential homes. To illustrate how apparent this distinction generally was, consider the gulf between 'feeling close' to a member of staff in a children's home, and taking your foster carers' surname as your own and calling them Mum and Dad.

Of the 39 interviewees in this study, a total of 30 had been in foster care. Of these 30, just eight had only ever been in foster care, whilst the rest had also experienced care in a residential setting. Two interviewees had been fostered by a relative during their care career. Generally speaking, young people painted a more positive picture of foster care than they did of life in children's homes, although there were several tales of previously positive placements that had later turned sour and broken down. To reiterate a point made in the previous chapter, it was clear that foster care was not appropriate for everyone.

> Foster placements weren't for me, it's just, it was *their* family, it was like their own family, their own thing they do it. If I didn't do their thing I'd either get locked out 'cos I wasn't allowed to stay in the house on me own. It was either you're locked out or go and see your dad, whichever. (Andrea, aged 16)

As Wilson *et al.* (2004) note, the strengths of foster care need to be balanced against its difficulties. For example, the backgrounds of young people can make it difficult for them to trust or settle with foster carers and there may be potentially difficult relationships between foster family and birth family. However, given that this chapter is concerned with the development of secure attachments, it is the more positive experiences of foster care that will be explored in some detail.

One thing that clearly hindered many young people's chance of finding stability in care was constant movement between placements, which was often unsettling and disruptive. Just two of the 39 interviewees had experienced one placement in care, whilst 24 had had four or more placements. The placement number of four individuals went into double figures! Those who move continuously are clearly less likely to develop quality relationships with their carers, if only for the fact that they are rarely in one place for long enough.

The development of quality relationships between young people and their carers is obviously a two-way process – dependent on both parties being willing and able to at least try to establish some degree of mutual respect. It is well documented that lack of attachment in children can take various forms (e.g. Ainsworth *et al.* 1978), but it is important to remember that carers have their part to play too if any level of attachment is to develop (cf. Sinclair and Wilson 2003). One of the questions asked of young people in this study was what they thought makes for a good carer.

> Someone who treats you as their own, who'll do things with you and sit down and listen to you if you're upset and stuff like that. Someone dead loving really. (Cath, aged 17)

> Someone who cares for the child, that's all they need, someone who cares for the child. And…say they got bullied or they did something wrong. Before having a go at them, you know sending them to bed or something, just think in their heads what they've gone through. And then talk to them if they've got something on their mind. They could have something on their mind that they've never talked to nobody about, so they're taking it out on other things or getting done by the police for it. (Billy, aged 16)

The most common responses to this question illustrated that what young people wanted most was simply to be cared for, listened to and understood. In addition, there was a desire to fit in and be treated normally, in the same way that carers treated their own children (cf. Wilson *et al.* 2004).

Developing secure attachments

In this study the stories of ten young people (just one of whom was male) suggested that they were securely attached to their carers. None of these young people was in custody at the time of interview. The assessments of attachment are based on self-reports by young people of closeness to carers. These assessments relate to whether there was someone special who cared about the young person and whom he or she in turn cared about, a carer who provided a secure base and emotional availability, someone the person could trust and whom he or she cared about letting down. Such relationships were generally evident when young people reported feeling 'part of a family', regarding carers as parent figures.

A significant theme to emerge from their stories, and indeed from the literature on attachment, is that developing secure attachments in the context of care is not a straightforward process. As Schofield *et al.* (2000) point out, children who have experienced poor parenting or been mal-treated, the experience of most although not all long-term fostered children, are likely to have an insecure attachment pattern. For example, they may well be anxious and negative about their own self-worth and the availability and reliability of others.

Insecurely attached individuals tend not to begin relationships at the same baseline as most other people. They start some way below the baseline and therefore have a lot further to go in order to establish secure attachments. Given that so many young people entering care do have insecure attachment patterns, it is perhaps surprising that as many as ten people in this study appeared to be securely attached to their foster carers. This seems to be quite a high figure, but may be explicable in part by the snowballing technique adopted in order to access interviewees.

This resulted in my being put in contact with several long-term foster carers who had been fostering for many years. The young people whom they knew who were old enough to participate in an interview (16 years old or above) tended to be those who had kept in touch and developed some level of attachment. Having said this, not all the 'attached' group had been accessed via foster carers. Consider Jenny's story for example.

Jenny (18) was placed in care with her younger brother when she was aged 15. Her mother has mental health problems, and Jenny says going into care was something that she wanted.

> It was a real relief to sort of not have any responsibility, because I was sort of acting as a parent over my mum and my brother, so it was really, really nice to move into care… I was completely mothered by my foster mum which was lovely.

She stayed in her first placement for a year, and during this time became very close to her carers.

> My carer was the number one person to me, got on really, really, really well…both the mum and the dad, I just took them on as my parents really, and their son. It was brilliant, it was really warm… you know anything that we wanted to do they'd come with us and support us, like doctors, dentist, anything silly like that they'd be there for us… It was really good, just really caring people there.

Later on in the interview I draw Jenny back to the subject of her relationship with her carers.

> Claire: Were you ever bothered about what your carers thought of you, in terms of upsetting them or letting them down?
>
> Jenny: Yeah, that was a big thing with my first carers, because I was going through counselling, which was obviously talking about everything that had happened at home. There were a lot of things that were dredged up…and they were getting very upset because I was self-harming, taking drugs and stuff, and that was really hard for them to take. And errm basically she used to cry in front of me, and that was sort of the first thing. So I just sort of said 'I can't live here any more' 'cos of that. I mean I realised it was only because she cared for me but I couldn't take it at the time.

Jenny was then moved to a second placement that she did not enjoy. She notes that the new carers were very inexperienced, and had no idea how to deal with all of the problems that she inevitably brought with her. At 18 she has now left care and reports that she is not in touch with her last carers. Yet she has remained in constant contact with her first foster parents: 'I've now sort of got a second family really, because even though it broke down in the first carers I still go back there.'

If we take 'sensitivity to the opinion of others' as a definition of attachment (Hirschi 1969), then Jenny certainly appears to be displaying all the right signs. She notes that she was unable to deal with the fact that her behaviour was causing her foster mother some considerable distress. Certainly it is an interesting idea that a foster placement may break down because the young person and their carer care about each other too much. In fact, in three of the ten cases of securely attached individuals, a good placement had broken down and then the young person had returned at a later date to re-establish contact.

Jenny only lived with her first foster carers for just over a year. This might seem like a relatively short time in which to establish a strong relationship. However, in her case it seemed that all the appropriate conditions were in place almost immediately. Unlike many young people, going into care was something that Jenny really wanted. She was glad to be living with foster parents and welcomed being mothered and being allowed to act like a normal teenager, and it seems that her foster carer was happy to mother her. In such circumstances there seems to be no reason why a quality attachment would not develop fairly quickly. However, for other young people, attachments to carers tended to develop over a longer period of time.

Growing up in foster care

Whilst long-term foster care has rarely been seen as a positive option, some have suggested that it may be a significant group of children's best chance of experiencing a secure family life (Schofield 2003; Schofield *et al.* 2000). This was a finding reflected in the stories of several interviewees who had been in long-term care.

Carol (27) went into care when she was aged five. After some short-term residential placements, and returning home in between, she and one of her sisters were placed in a short-term foster placement when Carol was seven. Their mother was a drug addict, and they were always told that they would return home once she was 'better'. The foster placement was planned to last for six weeks, but Carol ended up staying for 13 years! She left when she was 21. Below Carol talks about living with her carers, Lynn and John.

> Carol: Lynn was quite good, she treated you as her own. Some foster parents do and some people don't, and we was very lucky. She had a big family as well and she really didn't have to have us. It was nice to be treated as a family… We just sort of felt really comfortable, you know you was

always made to feel comfortable. And after the years it was like 'Oh you look like your dad', and it's like 'That's not my real dad', you know it was really funny.

Claire: So you're totally part of the family then?

Carol: Yeah, we always were, we never really felt like an outcast. We was always treated equal.

Although Carol left Lynn and John's to go independent when she was 21, she notes that they still see each other every week. Carol has taken Lynn and John's surname as her own.

Louise (26) is Carol's younger sister. She left Lynn and John's house when she was 19 and moved in with her fiancé. Louise had Lynn and John at her wedding and also at the birth of her second child.

Claire: What would you say the best thing about being in care is?

Louise: My foster mum. My children don't know their real grandparents, as far as my kids are concerned Lynn and John are their nanny and granddad.

One particular point made by Louise concerns her annoyance at being moved in and out of care so much when she was younger. She recalls being constantly told by Social Services that they would be returning home to their mother at some point, even when they moved to Lynn and John's. This made it difficult for her to settle down at first.

Indeed, Minty (1999) has recently questioned whether the policy of short-term admissions to care is always in the child's best interests, as it may have encouraged the 'oscillation' of children in and out of care with the result that some long-term admissions are simply postponed. Louise's story seems to reinforce this argument. Interestingly, constant movement in and out of care also characterised Chloe's early care experience.

Chloe (18) and her younger sister first went into care when Chloe was five. Their mother was mentally ill, and they were placed in short-term respite care on and off for six years. On one occasion when Chloe was 11 the respite foster carers were away, so Chloe and her sister were placed with Sally and Doug for the weekend. They ended up staying for seven years! Chloe herself remarks that living in long-term foster care has been so much better for her than had she continued moving in and out of short-term care.

> I used to have to look after my mum and my little sister, and never went out and didn't have any confidence. Then when I came here I didn't have anything to worry about, so I can get back to being my own age. It's just built up my confidence, just totally different to what it would've been if I'd kept on going to Jane's [the respite foster carer] and then to my mum's.

Clearly for some young people, long-term placements in foster care offer a real opportunity to develop strong and secure attachments (Schofield 2003). Louise's comment about her foster carers being nanny and granddad to her own two children indicates how long-lasting secure attachments can actually be, potentially spanning across generations. It is noteworthy, however, that Carol, Louise and Chloe's placements were originally intended to be short term. That their placements ended up being successful in the long term may have been as much down to chance as good social work planning.

Normal family life

Possibly one of the strongest indicators of secure attachment is when being in care doesn't actually feel like being in care, but feels like home. When interviewing individuals who had developed particularly strong attachments, I discovered that some of the standard questions that I tried to ask everyone were simply not appropriate. In some respects they were outside of the interviewees' own understanding of their experience.

Claire: How do you think being in care has affected your life?

Carol: I don't think of it as being in care, I think of it as being normal and part of a family. Lynn treated us normal, did our hair for us, loved us and pushed us to do well.

Claire: What would you say is the best thing about being in care?

Gill: Errm I don't really know, I guess living with Kate and Peter really. But I think it would be very different if we were somewhere else... I think a lot of foster kids get treated a lot more like they're being fostered than they're part of the family. We're just a family so it's different. So I don't know, it doesn't really feel like I'm in foster care, which is a bit strange.

As Chloe explained, when you've lived somewhere for a long time and you become part of the family, your whole way of thinking about the situation tends to change.

> Once you've been somewhere so long they become, I would never ever call Sally 'Mum' and 'Dad' because I've still got my mum and dad, but you do think of them as still your parents, your parent figure. So yeah you are bothered about what they think, but then after a while you know you're just part of the family, so you don't think 'Oh I wonder if they think I'm all right or not' like when you first come, 'cos you don't think like that any more. (Chloe, aged 18)

Chloe's comments also draw attention to one of the potential dilemmas facing those in long-term foster care, reconciling where your carers (who may well be your parental figures) stand in relation to your birth family (cf. Schofield *et al.* 2000). Most of the young people who had developed secure attachments to carers appeared to have dealt with this issue. For example, Chloe notes that whilst she does not call her carers 'Mum and Dad', she still thinks of them as her parents. Similarly, Carol stated that although she had taken Lynn and John's surname, she never called them Mum and Dad, because none of their own children did either.

A further dilemma that may face some young people in foster care is the issue of divided loyalties. Some individuals feel that they are being disloyal to their birth parents if they get too close to their carers and too comfortable in the foster home. On the other side of the coin, few birth parents find having a child in care desirable and may, in some circumstances, put pressure on their child to return home. This is what happened to Greg (18), who did not develop any secure attachments in care.

At the time of interview Greg was finishing a year-long custodial sentence. He had been in and out of care from the age of 11, and had experienced a variety of different placements. Although he did not enjoy his care experience overall, he notes that he got on particularly well with one set of foster carers:

> Greg: I got on with them, I were gonna go to Spain with 'em about a week before I went back to my mum. But my mum gave me a choice, she was getting to the stage where she was saying 'You come back to me or you don't come back at all'. So I went back... She was saying they were trying to take her place if you know what I mean, and she

was really jealous, which is normal I guess. Like I said to her, 'Well I'll come back to you'. I can't choose them over my mum 'cos my mum comes first.

Claire: But did you feel like you were at home with the foster parents, if you were going on holiday with them and that?

Greg: No, it was like a life that I would want if they *were* my family like, it was kind of cosy if you know what I mean. I went to school and everything, I got back in [to] education, I was gonna get a job, doing all that, then I went back to my mum and it all fell through.

Greg rejects the suggestion that he felt at home with his foster carers but notes that they gave him the kind of life he would want if they *were* his family. His story illustrates the conflicting emotions that can beset young people experiencing a positive foster placement. At age 15 Greg returned to his home environment having had just a taster of secure family life. Sadly, he never went back to school.

Positive experiences and self-image

Amongst those who were lucky enough to experience care as a secure base and develop strong attachments, there was a general feeling that going into care had been a positive turning point in their lives.

Had we not been placed with Lynn, I dunno what would have happened to us... It did us a favour going into care 'cos of what our life was like before. I'd have probably ended up like my mother, pregnant at 16 and into drugs. (Louise, aged 26)

I am glad I went into care...you get to realise what a normal family is like... If I hadn't gone in care I might have turned out like my family, treated my kids in the same way. (Laura, aged 19)

Note the emphasis above on *not* following in the footsteps of birth family members. A determination not to repeat the behaviour of parents was evident in the stories of several young people. As Melanie (20) noted, 'I've seen him on drugs, so that frightens me, I don't want to be like that... I'd rather be in control of what I'm doing.' Many felt that their care experience had helped them to turn their lives around, in terms of achieving things that they could not have achieved at home. Helen's (18)

story below places her foster carer firmly at the centre of the achievements in Helen's life.

> Helen: If I was still living at home I wouldn't have a job, I
>   wouldn't have gone to college, I wouldn't have got
>   through school, I wouldn't have done all of them.
>
> Claire: So what has it been about the care system, what's
>   changed?
>
> Helen: Well it's more the foster parents really. I mean Trish took
>   me into her home and treated me as one of her own kids,
>   which made me trust people…she's one in a million she
>   is… She's just like a second mum really.

It is well documented that various protective mechanisms can enable
young people to overcome previous psychosocial adversity (Rutter *et al.*
1998). One particular mechanism that may enable resilience is that
which opens up positive opportunities and turning points in life (Howe
et al. 1999). The stories above indicate that, for some young people, the
care experience can act as a very positive turning point. As Helen's story
suggests, the development of quality relationships with carers tends to be
a crucial aspect of this turning point. In their study of 472 foster
children, Sinclair and Wilson (2003) also found that the interaction
between child and carer was a key issue associated with successful placements. In particular, they suggested that placements were most likely to
be positive when children wanted to be fostered and carers were warm
and child-oriented.

An additional protective mechanism that has been identified in the
literature on resilience involves the promotion of self-esteem through the
development of secure and supportive relationships (e.g. Howe *et al.*
1999). In the current study it was very noticeable that those who had
developed a secure attachment in care were most likely to have a positive
self-image. Although I did not ask interviewees specifically about how
they perceived themselves, several volunteered information on this
subject, noting how they had changed as a result of being in care. Sarah
(17) noted: 'It's built up my self-esteem, my confidence. I'm just a whole
totally different person. I could talk to you for hours!' And Jenny (18)
said: 'I wouldn't be the person I am today if I didn't go through
everything I've been through… I just feel a very confident, really good
person.'

The above descriptions can be contrasted with the words of young people who did not develop secure attachments. These were individuals who had not experienced care as a secure base and regarded their care career in generally negative terms. Kate (25), for example, described herself as a very 'bitter' young woman.

> On one hand I've become a very tough person, I've handled everything that has come my way, and survived. On the other hand, after a few years of leaving care my toughness seemed to slowly disappear. I have suffered bouts of extreme depression, self-loathing, have been suicidal on many occasions... I've mixed in bad company, abused most of the drugs on the menu for many, many years. Had on-and-off counselling, been on anti-depressants... I have only come off the anti-depressants in the last six months, and no longer use drugs.

Liz (17) was moved in and out of care from a very young age, and has experienced constant rejection from her parents. She recalls a time when she was living with her father, and he just left the house one day never to return. She notes that she did not even cry, but simply went to live with her mother. She said: 'People call me a heartless so and so, but I just don't care. I don't care about anything no more.'

During my interview with Greg (18), he remarked that he had had various interviews with psychologists:

> One of them has seen me in the past and he says my head's completely messed up, he said all kinds of things. I would say yeah, it is messed up yeah, it's bound to be 'cos I've moved all over and...it does mess your head up being in care and being in jail, all of it, altogether, it messes.

The contrast between the different self-perceptions that young people have is quite striking. It may be misleading to suggest that a positive self-image results purely from the development of a secure attachment relationship. However, a warm and supportive relationship can certainly lay the foundations upon which a positive identity can develop. As was noted earlier, a positive self-image can be highly protective against a range of life challenges and risks. It is perhaps not surprising therefore that many who regarded themselves in a negative light were in prison at the time of interview. Indeed, several of the interviewees in custody revealed that they had had a poor self-image prior to being locked up.

Trust and respect

In the criminological literature, secure attachments to law-abiding others have long been regarded as protective against offending behaviour (Hirschi 1969). In this study, seven out of the ten young people who were identified as securely attached had not been in trouble with the police. Yet many interviewees (23 out of 39) pointed out that it was easy to break the rules in care and get into trouble if you wanted to.

Recall the discussion in Chapter 4, where young people themselves acknowledged that residential carers had very little power to prevent residents from getting into trouble. Equally, many who had been in foster care felt that it was easy to break the rules if you wished to. When asking some of the securely attached individuals what would stop them from breaking the rules, respect for carers emerged as a common theme, as Jenny (18) noted: 'Just my love and respect for the carers that I was with.' And Laura (19) said that 'It's really important to find the right foster carers for kids… Respect for my carers would stop me getting into trouble, but if you don't have respect then you don't care.' Laura went into care at the age of 12. Her mother was unable to control her as she was getting into trouble and fighting all the time, and had been expelled from school. Although Laura's first foster placement broke down, her second one was very positive and she developed a quality relationship with her carer: 'I came to realise it's not so bad being good… When I did have a good placement I didn't fight, I didn't want to. I didn't have any reason to.' In addition to having respect for a carer, several individuals clearly felt a sense of fairness with regard to the rules and boundaries that carers had set. For example, Helen (18) noted that 'She hardly ever grounded you, she'd let you out to go where you like as long as you tell her, as long as you're back by the right time, then everything's OK with her.' Meanwhile, Gill (18) said that:

> There weren't any rules that were unreasonable. I was probably more free than when I was with my dad… But there were some real plusses… I was with someone like a girl my own age, I was with other people rather than sitting on my own all the time.

Others who had been in long-term foster placements recognised and appreciated the fact that carers had afforded them a certain amount of trust.

> I had the trust to go out and not get into trouble, they actually trusted me to do that… And actually said to me well if you're going to this place then make sure you go to that place, don't wander off anywhere else… I never got in trouble at the foster parent's. (Alison, aged 18)

Note the focus on the individual above; for example, the use of the word '*I*' and the emphasis on '*me*' – 'they actually trusted *me*'. This contrasts with several of the earlier descriptions of young people running wild in residential care, where young people often emphasised 'we' and 'us'. It is arguable that young people perceive themselves to be more individually responsible and more accountable for their own actions when they do not live in a large group in which offending is the norm, and when they receive individualised attention from carers with whom they live every day. In such placements, there are also likely to be fewer opportunities for following the crowd than there are in larger residential units, and fewer options for hiding behind the crowd in explaining away offending behaviour.

Speaking of her time in a short-term foster placement, Adele (19) commented:

> If you're told to be in on time then you're in on time, the time they give you. You don't just stay out …because you have more respect for them than in the kids' homes… There wasn't loads of kids there, there was just one or two of you…they done more for you.

Of course this all relates back to the importance of carer continuity and stability in care, summarised by Beth (19) below.

> I think you have more respect for people that you see every day and it's their home… I know foster has its downfalls as well, but at least there's that bit of stability there. You know you're gonna be with those people every day.

Discipline from someone who cares

A further issue of interest highlighted by the story of one securely attached individual was the effect of being disciplined by someone who cares. The description of this that follows contrasts sharply with comments made in Chapter 4 about pointless discipline in residential care, where '*being grounded meant nothing*' and staff had no control.

Like others, Melanie (20) talked about the importance of establishing mutual respect with her foster carer: 'When I didn't need to be disciplined she was very lenient with me. She'd let me stay out late and she'd give me the trust that I needed, in order to build respect for each other I think.' However, when Melanie did need to be disciplined, her foster carer had no qualms about taking appropriate action. Below Melanie describes in some detail the day that she received her first caution from the police. She was in town with another girl and they were browsing in an electrical shop. As the other girl picked up a laptop computer the alarm wire came out.

> That was it, it was in her coat and she was out the door and I was following behind her…it just happened so quickly, and we just ran for miles and miles, I was running, 'Please don't come behind me'. And then she met up with her brother, gave it to him for sixty quid and off we went with thirty quid in our pockets. And I thought 'Ooh that was great', you know what I mean, bit of running and just, I wouldn't have been able to do it on my own, not at all, I'm not that confident. But it did shock me, a lot of things, and then when Debbie found out I just confessed… She took me down the police station, which was the best thing she could have done, because if I'd have thought I'd got away with it, I'd have done it again. Because I'm not strong-willed enough, to have that thirty quid in my hand that easy, no problem. I would have done it again if she didn't teach me a lesson so she was good on that as well. She took me straight down the police and made me confess. And they said 'We can't do anything because the shop haven't reported it' [*laughs*]. I was like 'oh right'. So she went up to the shop and told them, so they reported it and then I got done [*laughs*].

Melanie seems to regard this incident as a turning point in her life.

> Melanie: You definitely need someone behind you showing you the way to go, because if I'd have stolen that computer two years previously they wouldn't have known anything about it, and I could have gone a completely different way. But because I was with Debbie, she stopped it, she frightened me. They even arrested me, put handcuffs on me and everything. I was like 'Ohhhh I don't like this at all', and then to see how much I'd hurt Debbie as well by doing it. Because she was in tears when I was having my photos done and my fingerprints and, I was just, just

watching her just broke my heart, I realised what I'd done and that I'd hurt a lot of people, not just myself. So to have someone strong behind you that's not just gonna say 'Right you're a soft case, we'll pat you on the head and send you off'. You need somebody to not just think 'Oh because they're in care we'll be soft on them', you need a hard word just like any other kid would I think.

Claire: So what you're saying I think, is it's important to have someone who you're worried about letting down or that you're close to?

Melanie: Yeah, someone that is important to you, definitely… because if you haven't got anyone around you that cares then you don't really care about yourself either. Because your self-esteem goes down because there is nobody there that cares for you, so why should you care for you? So it makes you need somebody, if you've got somebody that you can let down then it stops you from doing a lot of things I think.

Melanie's story has been quoted at length because it supports the whole secure attachment argument so forcefully. Interestingly, her story also provides support for Braithwaite's theory of reintegrative shaming (1989), which states that shaming and punishment are possible while maintaining bonds of respect (and that doing nothing in response to an offence is likely to make matters worse).

Melanie's emphasis on the importance of having someone who cares also reiterates many of the comments made in the previous chapter, whereby young people felt that they were free to 'deviate' because there was nobody who cared. If individuals feel that nobody is bothered about them, they in turn may feel that there is nobody for them to be bothered about, nobody whom they should worry about letting down. Being enmeshed in secure and supportive relationships can raise young people's self-esteem while making them more sensitive to the opinion of others. This is regarded as highly protective against offending behaviour. Therefore, we may surmise that young people who are securely attached to their foster carer are less likely to become involved in offending behaviour and less likely to end up in prison. This, however, is not always the case.

A different case

The one young man in this study who was identified as being securely attached has a somewhat different story from those that have already been told, and it is to his care experience that we now turn. Jamie (22) was made a ward of court when he was aged three, and placed with long-term foster carers with whom he stayed for about 12 years. This seemed to be a very positive placement. Jamie refers to these carers as 'Mum and Dad' or 'my step-parents' interchangeably throughout our interview and notes that he was 'given every sort of opportunity in this placement'. However, the placement broke down when Jamie was 14.

According to Jamie, he first started getting into trouble when he was about 13.

> That's when it actually hit home what being a ward of court really meant, I didn't belong to anyone... Got terrorised at school for being in care, taunted by other kids saying 'you've got no parents'. I retaliated and started getting into what I can only call narcotics.

Jamie was expelled from school, and began 'causing havoc' at home. He frequently played truant from the next school at which he was enrolled, and eventually his foster placement broke down. He was then moved to a second foster placement, but this broke down after several months and he returned to his original foster home. When this broke down again he went on to a third placement. Jamie failed the few GCSE exams he was put in for and moved to an independent flat when he was nearly 16.

At this point he began getting into heavier drugs and also petty crimes. He received a community sentence for burglary, then later started living rough and pushing and selling drugs. He ended up serving a lengthy custodial sentence. After leaving prison Jamie was placed in a shared house, but notes that his house-mate was into 'serious' drugs. He said: 'I started smoking brown [heroin]... I was addicted for about six or seven months, didn't care about my appearance or nothing.' Jamie then moved around various hostels before finally ending up on a personal development course run by an organisation for young people. The course tries to teach communication and team-building skills to a range of young people, including care-leavers, ex-offenders and drug addicts. Jamie fell into all three categories when he began the course, but notes that he was a 'recovering' drug addict by the time he left.

Having originally done the programme as a participant himself, Jamie now works full time for the young people's group and runs a personal development course in his area. He has led three teams on the course up until now and notes that his own past experiences help him to relate to the needs of other participants. He said: 'I get so much job satisfaction... I love the job, it's the one thing that's really turned me round.' As for his old foster parents, Jamie has re-established contact and notes that he sees his 'mum and dad' regularly, although he lives independently now. In his view they have always been there for him. He said: 'I lived with 'em most of my life and took their surname... I still go and watch footie with me old man.'

The reason that Jamie's story is outlined in some detail here is because it seems to represent a 'deviant' case in this study (cf. Silverman 2000). In other words, it does not quite fit with the other care experiences described. During our interview Jamie appeared to be strongly attached to his old foster carers, frequently referring to what his 'mum' had said about something, or what his 'dad' thought about a situation. He has taken his carers' surname as his own and notes that he lived with them for most of his life. Indeed, the fact that he was initially with them from the age of 3 to 14 indicates that he had grown up with this family. Yet how was it that the attachments that were developed in this positive, long-term placement did not protect Jamie against drug abuse and offending behaviour? What might be the difference between Jamie's experiences and some of the more successful placements that were discussed earlier?

It is possible that the bullying that Jamie experienced at school was severe enough to undermine his attachment to his carers. Recall that he mentioned being 'terrorised' at school, 'taunted' by other children who said that 'you've got no parents'. This was when Jamie was 13, around the same time that he says he suddenly realised what being a ward of court actually meant – 'I didn't belong to anyone'. It is quite probable that Jamie's experience of being bullied led directly to his feeling that he didn't belong to anybody. At this particularly vulnerable time in his life he began using drugs.

> Claire: Do you think you would have got into drugs if you hadn't been in care?
>
> Jamie: Yes, I lived in Kenfield, they were everywhere. At 13 it was just adolescence, but if you're in care you do tend to think 'No one's gonna give a shit'.

Jamie puts his involvement in drugs down to adolescence and his story suggests that at the age of 13 he had a very low self-esteem. His drug use did not help matters, as a year later he had been expelled from one school and had left the foster home where he had lived for nearly 12 years.

Another crucial difference between Jamie and most of the other 'securely attached' young people in this study is his poor educational achievement. Whilst not all of the other young people were roaring successes at school, all went on to college and were encouraged to do well. Jamie, on the other hand, failed all of his GCSEs and gave up on college after a short time. By truanting from school and continually getting into trouble, it is arguable that Jamie missed out on the valuable protective factor of education. In order for education to be protective, young people do not even necessarily have to be committed to their studies but simply involved in school life.

As Howe *et al.* (1999) suggest, school life has the potential to open up positive turning points in the lives of young people. For example, new skills may be acquired, supportive friendships may form and a non-deviant peer group may be joined. All of these things may promote self-esteem, but are of course dependent on young people actually being at school: 'Children who avoid, resist or scupper such opportunities not only miss out on protective experiences, but also increase their exposure to risks including social isolation, skills incompetence and academic failure' (p.260).

After leaving his long-term foster home, it seems that the first positive turning point in Jamie's life was participating in the personal development course. Jamie notes that he loves youth work and would like to get into drugs counselling at some point. He describes his work as 'the one thing that's really turned me round'. According to Howe *et al.* (1999), a sense of self-efficacy is a well-known resilience factor. 'A sense of achievement at any age is rewarding and boosting. Successful task accomplishments can also generalise so that people feel more confident about tacking other challenges' (p.258). It seems to logically follow that a sense of achievement will inevitably raise self-esteem.

Whilst it is important to remember that Jamie's story represents just one care experience, it is worth pointing out that his story supports the view that turning points throughout life can alter the course of life trajectories (Sampson and Laub 1993). In addition, his story relates to what Maruna (2001) identifies as a 'generative script'. According to Maruna, generative scripts facilitate the process of desistance; for instance, by enabling individuals to use their previously negative experiences in a positive light. Interestingly, Maruna suggests that the classic example is of the recovering addict who has a desire to help others suffering from drug addiction.

Jamie's experience also highlights the well-established link between drug use and offending behaviour. In the 1998/99 *Youth Lifestyles Survey*, Flood-Page *et al.* (2000) found that using drugs was the strongest predictor measured of serious or persistent offending amongst 12–17-year-old boys. Amongst my interviewees, drug abuse also emerged as a recurrent theme in offending behaviour. Research evidence from elsewhere suggests that young people in care and leaving care may be particularly vulnerable to using drugs as a coping strategy (e.g. see Ward, Henderson and Pearson 2003).

Returning to Jamie's story, one of the most important messages that we can take from this is that secure attachments on their own are not necessarily enough to enable resilience. Something extra may be necessary to protect individuals against offending behaviour. Borrowing from Hirschi's social control theory (1969) it is arguable that attachment must be combined with some level of involvement in school life and/or commitment to education in order to be protective. The importance of education will be explored in Chapter 6.

Different kinds of attachment

Before concluding this chapter it is important to make some brief comments on different types of attachment relationship. First, let us remind ourselves of the kind of attachments that a few young people developed with residential carers. Recall that five young people spoke of feeling close to residential carers. Three of these individuals were able to name one specific person with whom they had got on particularly well. Interestingly, for two young people, these relationships became stronger because young people remained in contact after leaving the children's home where staff worked.

For example, Liam (26) had kept in touch with one residential carer for over ten years, although she had only worked in the children's home where he lived for about four months. Her family had even given him a key to their house:

And now I've got me own key to the house, turn up there when I want. It is sort of like a second home really, so I was quite lucky there. I mean…there wasn't many people I could get on with.

Liam's discussion of this relationship suggested that, of all the young people, he had developed the strongest attachment to a residential carer. However, this seemed to be a slightly different sort of relationship from that developed by those identified as securely attached. Earlier it was noted that the levels of attachment to carers that were reported in this study tended to be on a far deeper level in foster care than they were in residential homes. Those who established attachments with residential carers tended to do so as a result of keeping in contact over a period of time, rather than through the residential care experience itself.

The second point to be made in this section is that just because some young people do not develop attachments to their carers, it does not necessarily mean that they are unable to develop any attachments at all. Indeed, young people who are looked after often retain attachments and loyalties to family and friends, and this is one of the reasons why some young people prefer residential care to foster care (see e.g. Triseliotis *et al.* 1995). Whilst this chapter has focused on the relationship between young people and their carers, it would be possible to write a completely different chapter about other sorts of attachment relationship that young people described, for example, to their partners and their own children.

According to Sampson and Laub (1993), attachments formed in later life can sharply mitigate criminal activity. In this study several of the young people in prison at the time of interview noted that being attached to someone 'on the out' certainly affected the way in which they experienced their custodial sentence.

Below Donnie (19) describes how having a girlfriend has altered his perception of life in a young offender institution.

I just want to get out there to me bird really…'cos she don't want me in here all the time, it's doing her head in. It's doing *my* head in. It didn't used to do my head in, it used to be like care, if you know what I mean, when I first started coming to jail. It used to be like 'yeah, I'm back in care' kind of thing. But now, this time I've actually realised what it's there for…it's there to take you away from your loved ones.

Meanwhile Jackie (18) talks about being separated from her son.

> It's like I've been in prison all me life…from the children's home there's not really much difference from here… I don't mind it, I mean I hate it at the moment because I just wanna be at home and with me son. But that's the only thing. I mean if I didn't have me son, or anything like that, and if I didn't have a place to live, then you know it would be the next place to home really for me.

Interestingly, the experiences of Donnie and Jackie suggest not only that they are attached to their partner and child respectively, but also that they have developed a very different sort of attachment – attachment to an institutional way of life. Evidence suggests that some young people who have lived in institutional care may find comfort in the familiar surroundings of jail (see Carlen 1987). This issue will be picked up again in Chapter 7.

Summary

This chapter has explored how far it is possible to develop secure attachments in the context of care. The stories of young people have been used to illuminate the fact that even those placed at a relatively late age can develop quality relationships with their carers, sometimes in quite a short period of time. Ten young people were identified as being securely attached to their foster carers, most of whom regarded these carers as parental figures or 'Mum and Dad'.

Generally speaking, young people's stories suggested that it was far easier to establish respect and subsequently strong attachments in the context of foster care. The close relationships that did develop with residential staff seemed to be on a very different level from those with foster carers, and were not regarded as secure attachments.

Those who had developed secure attachments in foster care tended to reflect on their care experience in positive terms, and several young people commented that they felt they were better people for being in care. It has been argued that secure attachments can enable resilience to previous psychosocial adversity by promoting an individual's self-esteem. Such attachments may also be strongly protective against offending behaviour.

The following themes were evident in young people's accounts of how they came to avoid getting into trouble:

- having respect for a carer
- perceiving the rules and boundaries in care as fair and reasonable
- appreciating the trust that carers afforded them
- feeling individually accountable for their own behaviour to carers in whose homes they lived every day.

One young woman also commented on the effect of being disciplined by someone who cares.

Of the ten young people identified as securely attached, just three had been in trouble with the police. However, the story of one young man highlighted the fact that something more than attachment alone may be required to protect individuals. It is possible that involvement in school life and/or commitment to education are also important requirements. This idea will be considered in the following chapter.

Chapter 6

Experiences of education

Introduction

In the year 2000 the first ever national statistics on the educational qualifications of care-leavers were published (DH 2000). Up until this point,
the relationship between experiences of care and poor school performance had very much been taken as given. The new national figures not
only served to reinforce the view that many young people who had been
in care fared poorly at school, but arguably also highlighted that the situation was worse than many had imagined. They showed that 70 per cent
of young people in 1999/2000 left care aged 16 or over without any
qualifications. By 2003 this figure had dropped to 56 per cent (DfES
2003c), indicating some progress in raising the educational attainment
of children in care. However, the proportion of care-leavers obtaining
five or more GCSEs graded A*–C (or equivalent) continues to be very
low. The figure currently stands at about 6 per cent compared to a
national average of over 50 per cent for all children (DfES 2003c).

A recent report by the Social Exclusion Unit (SEU) highlighted that
low educational attainment is an important cause of the social exclusion
suffered by so many care-leavers in later life (SEU 2003). In addition, the
report noted that too many young people in care spend time out of
school. Given that low educational attainment and school non-attendance are important risk factors for offending behaviour (Rutter *et al.*
1998), a focus on education forms an essential part of the analysis in this
study. The aim of this chapter is to explore the impact of education upon
young people's lives. Whilst some consideration will be given to the
number of qualifications that young people claimed to have, there will
also be an important emphasis on how far being in care may differen-
tially affect educational experiences. In the previous chapter it was suggested that something more than secure attachments to carers may be

necessary to protect young people against offending behaviour. Could this 'something' be a good education?

Educational attainment

One third of the young people (13 out of 39), two of whom were male, had obtained GCSE or GNVQ qualifications. This group of 13 covered a wide range of achievements, from one young person with a grade 'G' GCSE, to another with 11 GCSEs, two A-levels and the offer of a university place. It is noteworthy that although several other young people spoke of 'flunking' their GCSEs, a significant number had in fact been unable to take their exams in the first place. The majority of this latter group had not been in school for a variety of reasons that included being pregnant, being in prison, being unable to get to school, looking after parents and waiting to find a school to attend. The continually assessed coursework element of GCSEs in particular generally requires young people to study in the same place over a period of two years. This is not always possible for young people in the care system who may find themselves moving between schools as they move between placements.

In addition to the 13 young people who had obtained GCSE or GNVQ qualifications, a further two individuals had passed 'other' exams at age 16 – one in a pupil referral unit. Meanwhile, three young people who had taken no school-leaving exams had gone on to pass NVQ qualifications. In summary, 18 young people interviewed (five of whom were male) had obtained some kind of qualification. This left 21 out of 39 interviewees with no qualifications at all. Of the 21 individuals, one young person was aged 16 and serving a short custodial sentence before returning to a residential home in time to take her GCSEs. The remaining 20 had either failed their exams or not taken them in the first place. All of these 20 young people had been in trouble with the police and 18 of them were serving a custodial sentence at the time of interview.

Regardless of educational attainment and whether or not individuals actually enjoyed school, the majority of young people saw the value of education. Several young people suggested that children in care should get as much support as possible to enable them to have a good education, whilst others expressed regret at their own failure to obtain qualifications.

> I would have liked to have a better education…it's because I was moved around from place to place. GCSEs are coursework and stuff like that so I couldn't do it. (Liam, aged 26)

> [Care] should be centred around the education of the child… I think it should be made mandatory for children to stay in care…until 18, and possibly even afterwards as well, until they've finished their A-levels or any education, you know further education that they're doing. (Jenny, aged 18)

The suggestion that young people in care should receive continual support and encouragement with their education, particularly when moving between placements and between schools, emerged as a common theme. Even those who acknowledged that it was their own choice not to attend school also stated that, with hindsight, they wished they had been pushed more. Jenny's suggestion that care should be centred around the education of the child neatly summarises several of the comments made.

Experiences at school

Experiences at school played a significant part in many interviewees' stories of going into the care system. For some, school may be a safe haven where young people can forget about their troubles at home. Yet, for many others, school is where behavioural problems may first manifest themselves or problems at home may become apparent to outsiders. Persistent non-attendance at school can alert teachers to the fact that there may be a problem at home, whilst young people's physical appearance at school can also cause alarm.

Louise (26) recalls how she and her sister were looked after by teachers at primary school when it became apparent that they were being neglected at home.

> The teachers used to shower me and Carol at school. They let us use the school showers, gave us clothes from lost property and they could tell we weren't eating. I think it was probably them who got Social Services involved.

Gail (17) also describes how her physical appearance at school led to Social Services becoming involved in her life. At 15 she was being beaten up by her step-father and attending school covered in bruises.

Unable to cope with everyone else's reaction to this situation, she stopped going to school and was subsequently admitted to care.

> I went to school up until the fifth year, about four months it was before me examinations. Because of me dad hitting me and everything, when I was going to school I was getting like grief off everyone, saying 'Oh no, does your mum let your dad hit you and hit the kids?' and all this. And it just got too much. I was just getting too stressed out with it all. So I stopped going to school, I explained the situation, the teachers already knew the situation and they knew that everyone had heard about it... So I stopped going because I couldn't cope with it any more, I was getting too upset and annoyed at myself... But I wish to god I hadn't stopped going because I was doing really well, 'cos I'd done me mock exams and I got really good grades, you know.

In a different way, Andrea (16) also found that problems at home were making it increasingly difficult for her to cope with going to school. She stopped going to school at age 13 and was first admitted to care in the same year.

> I went through first year and I was in all the top sets and stuff like that...then me dad started getting sick. He's got mental health problems and depression. So I stopped going to school to look after him. What was happening was I was getting up, making his breakfast, making my breakfast, getting ready for school, going to school, coming back, getting changed from school, going to get the shopping, cooking the tea, cleaning the house and then doing the same the next day. And it just got too much for me so I stopped going to school. Well I had days off school and then I started the odd weeks off school, and then I just completely forgot about it and just started looking after the house. It got too much for me and the house just started falling apart really, because we were around each other all the time and me dad's a bad alcoholic as well, which makes him even worse.

What the stories above have in common is that all of the young people's problems were being caused by the behaviour of others. For Andrea and Gail, problems at home led directly to their non-attendance at school and subsequent admission to care. However, other young people described how it was their own behaviour that led to them going into care in the first place. Many of the young men in particular had stories to tell of being in trouble at school.

Donnie (19) describes the frustration of being dyslexic. He was eventually placed in care after being expelled from two schools because of the trouble he was getting into.

> Basically, a teacher would come to you. 'I can't do this work Miss.' 'What, are you thick or something?' D'you know what I mean, 'cos that's the kind of school it was. And you got people round you what are doing their work. I'd just fold the desk, I'm not bothered. I go rampaging round the school…and I'd be that hyped up, I'm not bothered what I do. Because they're trying to make me do the work and I'm that pissed off with looking at it, and I can't do it. I cannot even read it.

Meanwhile, Simon (20) explains why he had stopped attending school some time before going into care. Like Donnie, he also appears to have had a poor relationship with his teachers. This was a common feature of the stories of those who had been expelled.

> They tried sitting me on me own, you know like in a corridor on me own with a table and all that… They didn't like me, the teachers, because I used to give 'em cheek… And I just walked out the school. Just walked out, thought I'm not sitting here like an idiot. I told me auntie and all that, and she understood because she knew they were just taking the piss making me sit there on me own.

With regard to school exclusion, one third of the interviewees (13 out of 39) reported having been expelled from school at some point. Indeed, recent data based on government outcome indicators for looked-after children highlight that they are more likely than other children to receive a permanent exclusion from school (DH 2003a). Furthermore, evidence suggests that young people who have been excluded are far more likely than their peers to have been involved in offending behaviour (MORI 2004). This was certainly true for the interviewees in this study. For some, disruptive behaviour at school seemed to be a first step on the road to involvement in crime.

Michael (18) was also expelled from school shortly before going into care.

> I was just, I was dead unsettled, I couldn't settle at that school. I mean I went to the school. I was there for like a year and a half, two years. But it was just…I dunno how to put it. I wasn't like getting into trouble with the police, I was just misbehaving, just hanging about and that all the time. And there was a little gang of us, and I always wanted to be the

leader, me. So I was like doing one better to get to the top. And I just carried on, carried on, until I was just going mad.

After being expelled and then placed in residential care, Michael described becoming very quickly involved in crime with fellow residents: 'Starting pinching cars, street robberies…it just escalated from there.' Clearly many young people were having problems at school before going into care, whether through their own behaviour or because of problems at home (of course it is quite possible that some people's bad behaviour at school was a reaction to difficulties at home). In light of this finding, let us now consider how far the care experience appeared to have an effect on young people's education.

The care effect

Ten individuals, all of whom were female, commented that being in care had had a positive effect on their education. Given that improvements at school rarely occur without a secure and stable placement, it is probably no coincidence that eight of these ten young women were identified as being securely attached to their carers in the previous chapter. Interestingly, for two young women, the improvement was simply that they were able to attend school once they had been placed in care.

Neither Helen nor Alison was attending school regularly when they lived at home. Alison (18) said: 'I was too busy bringing my brother up.' And Helen (18) noted: 'I used to love going to school, but my mum wouldn't let me go. She used to make me baby-sit.'

However, after being placed in care at age 12, Helen went on to pass all of her GCSEs and at the time of interview had just completed a two-year NVQ course at college. As for Alison, difficulties at school resulted in her attending a pupil referral unit, yet she still acknowledged the positive effect that her care experience had had upon her: 'My grades were getting better as well as my school reports. At the end I actually passed all of my exams, which if I had stayed at my dad's I wouldn't have passed none.'

For Jenny (18), being placed in care meant moving from a very stressful to a very supportive environment. She described how in addition to receiving support from her foster carers, the teachers at school who knew she had gone into care were also very helpful: 'The teachers that were around that knew about it I really really did get on with, and really respected and trusted… I just felt that I had a team of support at school as well. I've been so lucky really.' Jenny's positive comments serve as a complete contrast to the earlier comments about teachers made by Donnie and Simon. This reflects the finding that those who enjoyed school and who did not have disruptive behaviour and/or learning difficulties were more likely to regard teachers as an additional source of support.

The majority of those who felt that going into care had had a positive impact on their education had been able to stay in the same school and the same area. In general, they had experienced few placement moves whilst in the care system. In many respects, for these young people, going into care had not only removed them from a difficult environment at home, but had also helped to minimise the disruption in their lives. Sadly, this was not the case for everyone.

Thirteen young people felt that being in care had had a negative effect on their education. For most of this group, going into care may well have removed them from experiences of abuse and/or neglect at home, but their care careers were generally characterised by frequent placement moves, which resulted in school changes. Constant movement in care is of course very disruptive, and inevitably makes it less likely that individuals will experience care as a secure and stable base.

Billy (16) had been in care since he was five, experiencing six different placements. During this time he noted that he had been to three primary schools and two secondary schools. Below he talks about moving to his last school.

> I weren't very good at school...I got put in all the bottom sets when I started, without them looking at me records from me old school. I got put in all the bottom sets and it took them like a year to get me special needs sorted out. You know 'cos I needed special needs 'cos I've not been going through a lot of school. I've been going through a lot of things on me mind like. And then I didn't do very well, so I only had science and I didn't do very well in that. And I was meant to have a special person coming in and helping me out on that, you know talking it out, reading it out, but I didn't. So I got a 'G' on that, which was bad, but I don't really mind. If I could do that school life again I'd do it again, if I could do it again I would.

Given that Billy has been in care continuously from a very young age and his needs should have been very well known to the local authority, his comments about his failure to receive special needs support are particularly sad. Although this was not specifically asked about during the interviews, five young people reported having special educational needs in some shape or form. In the school year 2001/2002, 27 per cent of young people in care held statements of special educational needs, compared to three per cent of all children (DH 2003a). As these figures indicate, individuals in care are much more likely than their peers to require special needs support. In the interests of the young person it is obviously crucial that this support is organised as quickly as possible.

Melanie (20) was another young person whose care career had been characterised by instability – specifically eight placements and five school changes since the age of eight. She describes the effect of moving to a new school halfway through her GCSEs.

> I lost interest completely, skived for the first half of year 11… I used to forge my own notes… Having to fit into a new school at that age, it just didn't happen. I wasn't interested and they weren't interested in me, that's how I saw it at the time. So my GCSEs were just flunked basically, I didn't do very well at all.

Meanwhile, Beth (19) commented on the difficulties of attending school when she had been placed out of the area.

> I had to get up at silly-o'clock in the morning and get a train down to here… And then I got told off at school 'cos I was coming in like half an hour late every day, there was nothing I could do. I was getting the earliest train as it is, I can't do anything more than that, so I stopped going… I said 'I don't want to go school down here' and they said 'Well, why not'. And I said 'Cos it's like two or three hours I spend every day on travelling, you know. I can't get my homework done…' So they said 'Oh well, we'll try and get you a school down here'. But because I was 15 they then turned round and said 'Well there's no point, no school's gonna accept you at 15'. But they made no attempt to get me home tutoring to get me GCSEs, they did nothing. That was the one thing that really pissed me off and it pissed me off at the time. Even though school isn't brilliant when you're there, I wanted my GCSEs because I wanted to do something with myself.

If, as Jenny suggested earlier, care was centred around the education of the child, it is quite possible that the experiences described by Billy, Melanie and Beth could be avoided. Billy and Melanie had both experienced several moves in care. Whilst placement changes may be necessary and perhaps inevitable in some circumstances, it is of great importance that these changes be managed with minimum disruption to young people's schooling (cf. SEU 2003). As a general rule, it is arguable that school changes ought to be avoided where possible. However, Beth's story, which shows the difficulties of trying to attend the same school after being moved out of the area, is of course an exception. In their study of closing children's homes, Cliffe and Berridge (1991) found that almost half of the placement moves that they noted involved either a school change or serious transport difficulties.

Education in residential care

It is noteworthy that several young people who felt that being in care had had a negative effect on their education spoke in particular of how their education had gone downhill once in residential care. Recall Greg's comment in Chapter 4 that the staff in the home where he lived did not really care whether residents went to school or not, as long as they left the premises during school hours.

The Who Cares? Trust survey of young people in care (Shaw 1998) found that children in residential homes were less likely to be regularly attending school than those in other types of placement. The survey also drew attention to the importance of homework, noting that 'it is virtually impossible for a child who is unable to study outside school hours to achieve success or be entered for public examinations' (Shaw 1998, p.40). Just 26 per cent of respondents in placements other than foster care said that they were always able to find a quiet place to do their homework in their placement, with the books they needed and someone to help. Interestingly, the SEU recently highlighted a lack of support and encouragement with schoolwork at home as a major barrier to raising the educational attainment of children in care (SEU 2003).

The stories of children running wild in residential care, which were documented in Chapter 4, highlight that the residential care environment may not always be conducive to private study. Obviously this can create a serious difficulty for residents who do have homework that they wish to work on in the evenings. Admittedly, young people in the current study rarely mentioned homework. For some interviewees, it was simply their choice not to attend school in the first place.

As John (18) explained:

> The school was like built onto the houses where we used to live. And we used to have to go to school every morning, but we just used to jump

over the fence and go to the town centre pinching, or pinching cars…
We always used to get the porter saying we'd absconded and as soon as
the police seen us they used to take us back… We made an agreement
with them, if we go to school we get £5 a week or something like that
extra pocket money. Still never went though.

John's comments reflect previous themes already discussed in relation to
some of the reasons for offending in residential care. For example, highlighting the issue of living with other residents in an environment where
truanting and offending may be the norm, where young people who are
not at school have plenty of time on their hands during the day to
commit offences.

Rutter *et al.* (1998) suggest that 'truancy is a contributory risk factor
facilitating a drift into crime, possibly in part by providing additional
opportunities for misconduct' (pp.232–3). They further note that being
part of a peer group dominated by other low-achieving children is influential in explaining delinquency. It is possible to add to this that being
part of a peer group that includes children with knowledge about crime
is also influential.

In Chapter 4 John described being 'easily led' by older residents in
the children's home where he lived. He later commented with regard to
his education in residential care: 'I learnt nothing, not a thing… I learnt
how to pinch cars and burgle houses, nothing else.' Like John, Mark also
indicated that it was his own decision to give up on school. Mark (19)
had gone into care because of his own behaviour. He previously
explained his involvement in crime whilst in care as a consequence of
feeling that he had nobody to worry about and nobody was worried
about him. He returns to this theme when explaining his non-attendance
at school.

Mark: As soon as I got put in care I just stopped going to school.
Well when I was with me dad I was bunking off a few
times, like a couple of times a week and that, but as soon
as I got put into care, that's it, just stopped altogether.
Never ever went back.

Claire: Why did you not go back?

Mark: Same thing really, no one to worry about, like no one to
give you a lecture about it. Well I'd get a lecture about it,
but not like a parent.

Claire: Did you ever get hassled, like were you encouraged to go
            to school, by staff in the homes or your social workers?

Mark: Oh I was encouraged. Like I'd come home at about four
            o'clock and they'd know I'd not been to school…they'd
            just sit you down and say 'Look you've gotta go to school'
            and I'd say 'Yeah, ok, I'll go tomorrow'.

Claire: And it didn't happen?

Mark: No that was it.

For those like Mark whose school attendance was already on a down-
ward trajectory, entry into residential care did not appear to make any
difference to their education. If anything, it just speeded up the process
of non-attendance. In Chapter 4 Mark described going out shoplifting
and stealing cars during the day with others at the children's home
where he lived. It was noted that his behaviour had escalated towards
crime and delinquency after going into care. His comments on education
suggest that this occurred at about the same time as he stopped going to
school.

   As was documented earlier, many young people do have problems
with school prior to entry to care. Therefore, this should be an important
focus for improvement by the child-care professionals involved in their
lives. Although it was clear that some individuals had actively chosen not
to bother with school, others pointed to the very low priority afforded to
education in residential homes. According to Gemma (18):

Gemma: They just throw a couple of maths sheets in front of you
            in the kids' homes and say 'do that'.

Claire: Right, so you were being educated at the kids' homes
            when you were there?

Gemma: Yeah, but nobody ever done it.

Liam (26) was also critical of the education that he had received in residential care.

They've got a school on site, and it was just crap education. You'd go in
and you'd watch a video 'cos it was easier for the staff to put on a video
and let you do whatever. And that was it, that was about all you'd do,

there was just no learning whatsoever. And now, looking back, that's what really pisses me off, 'cos I wasn't stupid and I'm not stupid, but I had no opportunity… I mean there were exams at the end of it, just maths and English and I was like 'Can't I do geography and history as well?' They said 'No, you're the only one who wants to do it and we're not prepared to pay for a member of staff to sit there while you're doing an exam.' … I think I could have done a lot more with my life if I hadn't gone into care… I don't mind being a cleaner, I get good money. But I wouldn't be doing that if I had a proper education, I would have done a lot more.

Gemma and Liam's experiences of education in a residential home are undoubtedly a cause for concern. Of course it is important to acknowledge that many young people are already having trouble with school and education prior to entry to care. This may well be part of the reason that they have gone into care in the first place. However, the residential care environment previously described by interviewees, combined with the kind of staff attitude outlined above, suggests that once they are in residential care there may be little hope that young people will ever have the opportunity to improve their situation.

All children have a right to education under Article 28 of the UN Convention on the Rights of the Child (United Nations 1989), yet it appears that this right has not always been a priority for some residential care staff. The new National Minimum Standards for children's homes (DH 2002a) and fostering services (DH 2002b) will, one hopes, ensure that this right does become a priority for all children in care in the future.

Feeling different

Regardless of whether interviewees were doing well with their education or not, one common theme that emerged in many people's stories was the stigma attached to being in care. Just over a third of young people (14 out of 39) spoke of feeling different from their peers, and five reported having been bullied at school because they were in care. As Shaw (1998) notes, the stigma attached to being in care is often referred to by young people, and one place where this stigma is most likely to be felt is school. Feeling different from other pupils inevitably affects young people's educational experiences. As Jackie (18) explained, 'I felt different from everyone else 'cos I'd have to wait behind after school. They'd all walk off home, and I'd be sat there waiting for the taxi to take me back to the children's home.' Jackie went on to describe other people's reactions to her being in care.

Jackie: They look on you as though you've never had any love or care or anything like that... Because you've been in care and you haven't had a family doesn't mean to say you've not loved or cared for anyone.

Claire: Have you got any example of people being like that?

Jackie: Yeah, at school. One girl used to say I'm hard-faced because I didn't have a family to love me and care for me. But I just argued her back and just said 'What difference does it make where you are and what you do, as long as you know what love is and you can give it?'

As for Melanie, when asked what the worst thing about being in care was, she responded as follows: 'Feeling different, feeling different's a very horrible thing... At school no one knew I was in care, everyone used to think I came from a happy family, then one day someone found out and I was devastated.' Feeling different had also clearly had an impact on Gemma (18).

Gemma: I always felt abnormal, because you see other normal kids going to school in the morning and going home and walking back, and I just used to feel abnormal. And I cut my arms thinking why can't I not be normal like them [*at this point, Gemma revealed her severely scarred forearms to me*]. Why do I have to have a disruptive life?

Claire: Why did you feel like you were abnormal?

Gemma: Just being in a place like that, and everyone looking down on us like we were bad people.

Morris (2000) refers to the common labelling of children in care as mad or bad, which she rightly argues is a serious barrier to promoting the interests of young people in care. Gemma's story highlights the painful effects that such labelling can have upon individuals. The negative labelling of young people in care is certainly not new. In her 1979 study, Barbara Kahan drew attention to the fact that the 'children's home kids' tended to be regarded as outsiders by both staff and other pupils at school. However, feeling different is not just a problem for those in residential care.

As Sarah (17) commented:

> To be truthful, telling someone you're in foster care, they automatically pre-judge you... Once they actually get to know you, then you can tell them. That's what I feel...because they know once they get to know you that you don't lie, you don't nick, you're nothing what they automatically think.

Billy (16) had also experienced difficulties with other children at school.

> The kids don't understand, people my age, they don't understand. You could tell them and they could just take the mick... You know, they bully you and that, I got bullied all through my school life... They just think up something to call you, and they'd call it you. Something about being in care like. They said daft jokes like 'What do you drink at night?', you know, alcohol-wise, and they say 'Oh you drink Fosters!'

Most people want to fit in at school, nobody likes to feel different. Yet the stories above indicate that many young people in care not only feel different from their peers, but are also treated differently, as a result of being in care. As Morris (2000) notes:

> School can be an important source of continuity, friendships and feeling good about yourself. Or it can be a daily torture of isolation and bullying. Negative experiences like this will inevitably mean that children lose out in terms of education. (p.55)

Such negative experiences can also compound the insecurity and uncertainty that comes from many placement moves and subsequent school changes.

Learning in a young offender institution

In contrast to many experiences at school, feeling different as a result of having been in care did not appear to be an issue for young people in custody. In fact, several young people commented that many of their fellow-inmates had also been in care.

According to Donnie (19), 'Half the people what are in here were in care.' When asked how she had adapted to life in a young offender institution, Gemma (18) responded: 'Easily, because everyone I knew was in here, from the kids' homes. It was like a big family reunion!'

Whilst such comments indicate that the pathways between care and custody continue to be well trodden, it is worth noting that several young people appeared to be benefiting from some of the opportunities available to them in their young offender institution. Of the 20 young people in the study who had not obtained any qualifications, 18 were in custody at the time of interview. Yet many of these individuals spoke of doing some kind of education or course whilst in prison.

Amongst those in custody at the time of interview, 16 were involved in some kind of education. Interestingly, when discussing future plans, eight of the ten young women claimed that they were intending to go to college, compared to just two of the ten young men. Of course it is not possible to claim any statistical significance for such small figures. However, if we take a commitment to further education as a sign of possible desistance from crime and a desire to improve oneself (and this certainly reflects the stories of those who wanted to go to college), then this finding does fit with overall offending rates for men and women. Female offending rates are never as high as male rates in the first place, and females tend to 'grow out' of crime more quickly. According to the most recent official *Criminal Statistics*, the peak age of offending is 19 for males and 15 for females (Home Office 2003d).

It is not only traditional educational courses that are available in young offender institutions, but also self-help groups and courses on topics such as anger management and drug abuse. Several young people commented on the positive aspects of the overall educational opportunities that were available to them.

> The education is good, I must say. Because like you don't get prison certificates, you get like local college certificates so it doesn't reveal the fact you've been to jail. (Donna, aged 16)

> I'd never done a course like 'Crime and Consequences'... It went through the whole day before you did the crime. It learnt me a few things about what I were doing, that did. (Greg, aged 18)

> They've got an AA in here; Alcoholics Anonymous. I've been to that for about two months, and listening to other people, it helps, makes you understand. (Trisha, aged 17)

In some ways it may seem difficult to reconcile some of the positive accounts of education in custody above with the critiques of custody discussed earlier in Chapter 2 (e.g. Goldson 2002a). Perhaps the best way to explain this is to note that the overall custodial experience remains an extremely damaging one, and one that is, for the most part, entirely unsuitable for vulnerable children. However, many young people's exceptionally poor (or virtually non-existent) pre-custody education means that being forced to engage with some level of study or self-help in prison may be regarded as something positive.

Whilst Donnie (19) had not been involved in many courses, he described how time spent inside had enabled him, for the first time, to begin to overcome the difficulties of dyslexia.

> As I've come in here, I can write letters now perfectly, well not perfectly, but I can write them and people understand what they are. And I can read a book. Then, I could read a sentence from here to there, just one sentence, and I wouldn't know what the first word I'd just read was. You know, because I'm that slow at it. But now, I can read a whole book and I can remember what it is at the beginning. That's since I've been put in here and stuck in a cell on me own. I've had to do it if you know what I mean.

Adele (19) was doing her NVQ in painting and decorating. She planned to complete the course at college and go on to do interior design.

> Since I've been here…it's given me some good confidence to know that I am capable of going to college. Because I've been in the painting and decorating, and I *have* enjoyed it, and it's made me say 'Yeah, you can go to college, girl. If you can do it in here, then get out there and do it.'

Adele's story highlights the positive impact that educational opportunities can have upon young people. Success in education and/or task accomplishment can certainly help to promote confidence, self-esteem and self-efficacy (Rutter *et al.* 1998). For those who have previously failed to gain qualifications (i.e. most of the young offenders in this study), learning in a young offender institution may sometimes offer individuals a second chance and perhaps ultimately a fresh start for when they leave. However, it is of course up to individuals how far they take advantage of the opportunities available to them. Not all of the young offenders were quite so committed to their studies, as the following conversation with John (18) demonstrates:

John: I'm doing me GCSE in maths, but it doesn't look too
            good at the minute. I don't think I'll pass that, I've been
            missing lessons and tests and that.

Claire: How come you've been missing lessons?

John: Because I go to education, there's only like eight people
            that can go in a lesson, and there's about ten people. So I
            just wait until them all have gone in and I say to the
            teacher 'The class is full, I need to go into art or
            woodwork.' Them are good, I get a better lesson.

John's story highlights that some degree of motivation and commitment
is required on the part of the young people if they are to benefit from the
education on offer to them.

Self-motivation and commitment

Interestingly, several young people commented on the importance of
self-motivation when it came to education, going to college or even
trying to give up crime. Many people had experienced disruptive and
difficult care careers, with frequent moves between placements, and
these had inevitably had a negative impact on their education. However,
amongst those who were working towards various qualifications, there
was a recognition of the importance of taking control over their own
lives in order to achieve success. A sense of determination and commitment was evident in the comments made by several young people.

After Adele (19) had explained how studying in the young offender
institution had given her the confidence to apply to college, I asked her
whether she saw herself ever coming back. Her response was: 'No! I
know for a fact that I'm never gonna come back to prison again in my
life, never... I'm dead set on getting me career sorted out, giving me
baby all my time and being a good mum.' Commenting on the courses
available to inmates and whether the education could make a difference
to people's lives, Adele noted: 'It's down to the person isn't it...if they
wanted it, it could change 'em, if they wanted it that bad.' Dave (19) was
very positive about the range of courses on offer in his young offender
institution but pointed out: 'You can only be helped if you wanna be
helped.'

For Melanie (20), actually being committed to what she was doing had made studying a whole lot easier. Making a conscious decision about her career had also given her something to aim for.

> I decided to go back into nursing, which is something I realised whilst travelling that I really wanted to do... And now I'm doing my NVQ...and working at a rest home... It's a lot easier now, because I'm doing it off my own back, it's up to me, there's nobody behind me pushing me. It's just me saying 'Right, this is what I wanna do'.

Jenny (18) also emphasised the importance of pushing herself.

> I was really pushing myself the whole way through, because my mum is a very educated person. It just wasn't anything but options, getting rid of your GCSEs, A-levels and then going to university... I was completely self-motivated.

Gill (18) was the other young person in the study who was about to start university. She spoke about how she had changed as a result of being in care.

> Just everything made me think well I'm gonna go ahead with my life whether my parents want me to or not, which they obviously do, but they don't you know. I'm not gonna let them stand in the way. I'm just sort of more determined to think well I'm gonna be independent ...rather than just sort of get knocked aside.

At the end of our interview, I asked Gill whether she thinks her life has been better as a result of being in care.

> Yeah, it's not so much just my life 'cos that's pretty much stayed the same, it's just me really that's changed, changed for the better, which I'm sure you can relate to. You go in naïve, just not having a clue. And then you think I'm gonna get something out of life, dunno what it is yet, maybe it's just happy, but if I can ever get there then that'll be good!

There is certainly a sense of determination, confidence and commitment running through most of the stories above. Whilst Gill was fortunate enough to still be living with her foster carers, Adele, Melanie and Jenny had experienced some difficult times since leaving care, yet they had survived to tell their stories and were arguably stronger people for their experiences. All of the comments emphasise the importance of taking charge of your own life and trying to help yourself. Without some level of self-motivation or commitment it is of course very difficult to do well educationally.

However, it is important to add to these comments that young people also need encouragement, support and positive role models if they are to see the value of education in the first place. In this study, Jenny's remark about her mother being very educated was quite unusual. Many young people in care have not had such a role model to look up to, which is why it is so important that they receive consistent support and encouragement throughout their care career (cf. SEU 2003).

Does education protect?

Finally, let us consider an idea put forward at the beginning of this chapter and at the end of the last. How far does education protect against offending behaviour? Jamie's story, which was outlined in the previous chapter, highlighted that something more than secure attachment to carers may be necessary to protect individuals against involvement in crime. It was proposed that this 'something' may be involvement in school life and/or a commitment to education.

Of the ten young people who were identified as securely attached in this study, just three had been in trouble with the police, one of whom had served a custodial sentence. The nine females in this group who had not been to prison had either already been to college and obtained qualifications or were in the process of completing further education courses. Two of the young women were about to start university. Whilst not all of these young people were roaring successes at school, they had all been attending school for the most part and had been encouraged to do well. It was suggested that the difference between the nine females and Jamie (who was the tenth securely attached individual) was that he had missed out on the protective factor of education by continually truanting and getting into trouble.

As was noted previously, in order for school education to be protective, young people do not necessarily have to be committed to their studies but simply involved in school life. The opportunities to acquire new skills, make new friendships and join new groups at school are all potentially protective. However, if young people are absent from school they miss out on such opportunities and also increase their exposure to the risks of social isolation and academic failure (Howe *et al.* 1999).

In this chapter it has been noted that many young people who go into care are likely to have previously been absent from school for a variety of reasons. For example, they may have been looking after a sick parent, baby-sitting a sibling, avoiding the gaze of outsiders on their signs of physical abuse or simply truanting through choice. Once in care, many young people continue to miss out on large chunks of their education. This is frequently due to placement moves that result in school changes and compound the difficulties that young people may already be experiencing. As Michael (18) explained, 'There was never time for school. I was just getting moved everywhere, all over the place. There was never any time to do nothing really, except mess about.'

Some individuals find themselves waiting to find a school to attend; others find that they have been placed so far away from their school that it is virtually impossible to make it to school on time. Others still may have been expelled and are being taught in a residential care environment, which may or may not be conducive to private study and which may or may not employ staff with enough time on their hands to support and encourage young people in their learning.

On top of all this, those who are fortunate enough to have a school to attend may find themselves up against the stigma attached to being in care and the negative labelling that this stigma brings. Many young people in care report feeling different from their peers at school. Being bullied for being in care can only compound this situation. When we consider some of the circumstances that young people in care may face during their school career, is it any wonder that, as a group, they are nine times more likely than their peers to have statements of special educational needs (DH 2003a), more likely to truant and more likely to receive permanent expulsions?

Unfortunately, as has been seen, there are obvious links between school non-attendance and offending. As Greg (18) stated: 'I went to a school and like I said I got expelled from it, so I didn't bother going to school any more. I just burgled.' These links were often most evident when young people had lived in an environment with other children where truanting, offending and not having a school to go to was the norm. School non-attendance was also associated with instability in care. Conversely, the positive effects of experiencing stable placements were very evident in the current study. For example, serious conflict in the home resulted in Sarah's (17) entry into the care system, where she experienced a very positive foster placement: 'I really needed to get away for my GCSEs as I was telling you. 'Cos they didn't think I would get any good marks if I stayed at home, which I didn't either.' Once in care Sarah went on to pass eight GCSEs and was in the first year of an NVQ course at college at the time of interview.

Of the ten young people identified as securely attached to their carers, nine had obtained qualifications. Of the ten young people who felt that care had had a positive effect on their education, eight were identified as being securely attached. In Chapter 5, the positive self-images portrayed by many of the securely attached individuals were examined in some detail. It is highly possible that the impact of educational achievement had helped to promote young people's self-esteem.

We can explore this idea further by considering the self-images of those who had not obtained GCSE or GNVQ qualifications. When discussing lack of educational attainment, several interviewees commented on their own intelligence, although this was not something that I had specifically asked about.

According to Michael (18), 'The only thing I regret is not getting any qualifications, but I'm not thick.' As for Gemma (18), her words rather sadly indicated a very low self-esteem: 'I'm thick – very!' Meanwhile, recall Beth's words. They suggested a feeling of failure to achieve her full potential: 'Even though school isn't brilliant when you're there, I wanted my GCSEs because I wanted to do something with myself.' Indeed, many young people expressed regret at their failure to obtain qualifications. As Greg (18) stated, 'They should get people doing their education…'cos that's where I went wrong. I didn't do me education, I messed up… I've got no education, no qualifications or nothing.'

These quotes are quite a contrast to the confidence and determination that ran through some of the earlier stories told. There is little doubt that educational achievement can bolster young people's self-images, whilst academic failure often has the opposite effect. The latter is not only associated with social exclusion but is also a risk factor for offending. Of the 20 young people in prison at the time of interview, 18 had no qualifications. In the previous chapter it was noted that many of the young offenders seemed to regard themselves in a negative light.

A whole range of factors may be at play in influencing young people's behaviour. However, the above discussion has attempted to demonstrate that involvement in school life and educational attainment may be intrinsically related to secure attachments and a positive self-image in protecting young people against involvement in crime. In

Chapter 5 the importance of establishing secure attachments to carers was outlined in some detail. It is arguable that educational attainment is unlikely to occur unless young people experience care as a secure and stable base. However, security and stability alone are not necessarily enough to protect against offending.

Summary

Ten young people in the study commented that being in care had had a positive impact on their education, whilst 13 individuals felt that being in care had had a negative effect. Amongst the latter group, frequent placement moves and school changes were common. Although many young people were experiencing difficulties at school prior to entry to care, several noted that their education had gone rapidly downhill after being placed in a residential home. Comments made about the low priority afforded to education in residential care are particularly worrying.

It has been argued that involvement in school life and a commitment to education can help to protect young people against offending behaviour when they are also in a secure and stable placement. Educational attainment and warm and supportive relationships with carers help to promote self-esteem and are particularly important in enabling individuals to become confident and independent young adults. Unfortunately, a significant number of young people (20 out of 39) had neither obtained any qualifications nor established secure attachments in the context of care. On a more positive note, a small number of individuals had achieved some of the highest grades at school and at college.

Although it is important to acknowledge that some young people are disillusioned with or uninterested in school before they go into care, several of the stories in this study indicate that entry into care often does little to improve this situation. In some cases it can make matters worse, particularly in placements where truanting, offending and not having a school to go to are commonplace. Going into care may intensify educational failure in some young people and create it in others. This, in turn, may encourage offending behaviour. The protection of children and young people from harm is undoubtedly the ultimate priority for Social Services. However, if care were centred around the education of the child, as one interviewee suggested, many of the difficulties experienced by young people in this study could well be avoided in the future.

Whilst the education of children in care has been very seriously neglected in the past, there are some hopeful signs that this situation is changing (see SEU 2003). Indeed, it is encouraging to note that policy responsibility for children in care in England has recently shifted from the Department of Health to the Department for Education and Skills. Young people with qualifications are of course more likely to find employment after leaving the care system, and this may ease their transition to independence.

Chapter 7

Life after care:
Coping with independence

Introduction

In October 2001 the Children (Leaving Care) Act 2000 came into force, with the promise of extended support to care-leavers. With its aim of delaying the discharge of children from care 'until they are prepared and ready to leave' (DH 2001c, p.5), the Act certainly has the potential to improve outcomes for future generations of young people leaving care. However, it is important to recognise that extended support will only be available if local authorities are provided with appropriate resources to implement successfully the provisions of the Act. Therefore, this piece of legislation should be regarded as the beginning, and not the end, of a concerted effort to provide help and support to care-leavers.

This chapter explores young people's experiences of life after care, with a particular focus on the transition from care to independence. It is noteworthy that the stories told in this chapter are all of leaving-care experiences that occurred prior to the introduction of the new legislation – under the Children Act 1989. The difficulties faced by many young people leaving care, particularly those who have been forced into independence at a much earlier age than their peers, will be examined in some detail. However, there will also be some consideration of how far the provisions in the Children (Leaving Care) Act 2000 are relevant to the experiences of young people in the current study. If implemented properly, can the Act fill the gaps in provision and support identified by young people who have previously left care?

Age upon leaving care

In the year ending 31 March 2002, the number of young people in England leaving care aged 18 or over rose slightly to 3240. The vast majority of these young people (3200) ceased to be looked after on their eighteenth birthday. Meanwhile, the number leaving care at age 16 or 17 fell to 3400, a figure that has been continually falling since 1998 (DH 2003b). These trends seem to be moving in the right direction and suggest that, in line with government policy, fewer young people are being inappropriately discharged from care at age 16 or 17. Since the introduction of the Leaving Care Act, one would expect these trends to continue, with an increasing number of young people remaining in care until they are 18.

Of the 39 young people in this study, three were still in care at the time of interview. One individual had moved out of her foster carer's home at age 21, another at age 19. The remaining interviewees reported having left care between the ages of 15 and 18. Six young people left care at 15, three of them having gone directly from care to custody. Twenty young people had left care at age 16, two had left at age 17 and finally six individuals had left when they were 18 years old.

Several of those who had left care at 18 referred to their eighteenth birthday as a turning point in their lives. The majority of teenagers in the general population eagerly await the arrival of their eighteenth birthday and the newly acquired rights that this day brings. Yet for young people in care, the approach of this particular date is often dreaded because of what it signifies with regard to their status as 'looked-after' children.

Only one of the eight individuals who had left care aged 18 or over had served a custodial sentence, compared to 13 of the 20 individuals who had left care at age 16. This lends support for the view that leaving care early can increase young people's vulnerability to involvement in crime. However, it is important to note that a total of eight individuals reported having gone directly from a care placement into custody. It is therefore not possible to say that this particular group had experienced the kind of vulnerability associated with leaving care early.

Although some interviewees had left care in order to go to prison, and a few others had actively chosen to go independent at an early age, the majority of young people were very critical of the way in which Social Services dealt with leaving-care issues. This was true even for those who had experienced positive placements whilst in the care system.

> Social Services disowned me as soon as I hit my eighteenth birthday and I've got the birthday card to prove it. 'Good luck in life' it said. (Jamie, aged 22)

> I would have liked to have spent more time in care. I did actually get a panel to see if I could stay in care longer, but they refused it, because once you're 18 they wanna chuck you out. (Jenny, aged 18)

> Social Services were too quick to agree when I said I wanted to go independent at 15... I wasn't ready. (Laura, aged 19)

When discussing leaving-care experiences, words such as 'disowned' and 'chucked out' were frequently used. Several individuals echoed Laura's sentiments that Social Services were only too eager for them to leave care at an early age. Others noted that a certain amount of pressure was placed on young people to free up a placement when they reached the age of 16 or 17. This kind of pressure often results from the fact that care placements are a very scarce resource and social workers are under pressure themselves to provide accommodation for many children. However, the situation does little to make young people feel secure in their placements.

The Leaving Care Act places a new duty on local authorities to provide accommodation for 16- and 17-year-olds who are looked after. Yet without an increase in the number of care placements available, this will be difficult to carry out in practice. Although efforts are underway to recruit and retain more carers (cf. DH 2003c), the continually high turnover of staff in the social care sector represents a considerable challenge to improving the care system and to delaying young people's discharge from care. Furthermore, not all young people are ready to leave care at 16 or 17 and, as Jenny's comment indicates, some may wish to remain where they are beyond the age of 18 (cf. Stein 1997). Given this finding, it is disconcerting to note that, of the 6640 care leavers aged 16 and over in 2001/2002, a mere 40 had remained in care beyond their eighteenth birthday (DH 2003b).

Preparation for independence

Lack of preparation for independent living has been consistently highlighted as a difficulty facing young people leaving the care system (e.g. Stein and Carey 1986; Stein and Wade 2000), and is an issue that is addressed in some detail in the Leaving Care Act. The importance of learning about budgeting, domestic skills and other practical self-care needs was emphasised by many people in this study.

When asked if she had any preparation for independence, Laura (19) responded: 'No, they don't set you up for the real world, it was a real reality shock.' Mark (19) also noted that everything had been done for him whilst in care. He was placed in a hostel at 16.

> When I was in care I had all me cooking done, all me washing done. Didn't know how to cook, didn't know how to wash, didn't know how to get on housing lists. I was just lost really... I'd buy about five pounds' worth of shopping...and I thought 'Well this'll do', run out in about two days. Clothes starting shrinking in the wash and everything.

Whilst several young people who had been in foster placements noted that they had been expected to help with general household chores, many of those who had been in residential homes claimed that everything had been done for them. However, one young person who had been in residential care felt that her preparation for independence had been a little over-zealous, and certainly not appropriate to her individual needs.

Below, Beth (19) describes her experience of moving out of the children's home where she lived.

> When I was there they built an extension on the back of it, and that was like where you go to at 16, 17, you have to go into it and start being independent... It was a tiny little bed-sit and you know they said to me 'Right well you're not allowed in the building, you're allowed in like an hour a day, that's it... This is how it's gonna be, this is what it's like when you're out in the big wide world.' But I thought well it's not, you normally have your parents to support you, you can go round and have your tea if you feel like it... But they weren't having none of it, they used to lock the door and all sorts... And like they were saying 'Oh you're gonna have to learn to cook and clean for yourself' and I said 'Well I've been doing that for years, I don't need to learn to do it. That's why I came into care, to get a break from it all'... It didn't matter how many times I told them I didn't want that, they were just like 'Well it's tough, you'll have to move out at some point.' I was like 'Well I know that, but can't we make it a bit nicer while I'm here?'

Later I asked Beth if she had any choice at all about being moved out.

No, I refused to do it and I created a bit of a scene, and I ran away. And when the police brought me back all my stuff had been moved into the independence unit and the front door to the house was locked. So that was it, that was how I moved in.

Whilst preparation for independence is of crucial importance to young people in care, Beth's story illustrates the importance of taking account of individual needs and experiences. The policy of moving young people out of the main building and into the extension at 16 was clearly inappropriate for Beth. Furthermore, her views and opinions on the matter were apparently ignored. Several young people in this study commented on the fact that they felt they had very little control over their movement from care to more independent lodgings. Clearly, if young people are not being consulted about what happens to them then it is very difficult to know their needs, let alone meet them.

Under the Leaving Care Act, young people in care are required to have a Pathway Plan that helps map a route to independence. It is intended that 'each young person will be central to drawing up their own plan, setting out their own goals and identifying with their personal advisor how the local authority can help them' (DH 2001c, p.40). If this is achieved, the difficulties experienced by Beth and others could well be avoided in the future. However, Broad (2003) recently found that more than a year after the Act came into force, 27 per cent of the young people in his study who were entitled to a Pathway Plan did not have one, (although he also identified some improvement in the accommodation and financial services provided by certain leaving-care projects).

Several young people in the current study referred to the particular difficulty of managing their finances. One argument made was that the regular allowances received by individuals whilst in care did not help to set them up for the real world. Given that many young people in care come from a relatively poor background and may not be used to receiving much pocket money each week, the money they receive once in the care system can come as a pleasant surprise. Three interviewees felt that one of the best things about being in care was the money that they received each week.

Yet whilst pocket money, clothing allowances and travel money were all very welcome whilst in the care system, some of the older care-leavers acknowledged that it did not do to get used to having too much money to spend. As Laura (19) explained: 'The clothing allowance is too easy to blow at once… Carers should have more control over it, and maybe not give it all over at once.' Melanie (20) noted that there was a striking contrast between the money she had received whilst in foster care and when she was living in supported lodgings at age 16.

> I was getting about ninety quid a month off Social Services [in foster care], and then all of a sudden I'm on my own, I've gotta pay bills and sort myself out and buy food, and make sure I've got enough money for the whole month… It just got incredibly confusing. I was depressed for about a month.

As the comments above indicate, young people may be particularly vulnerable when making the transition from care to independence. In terms of the kind of preparation for independence that may be needed, young people in this study emphasised the importance of learning about budgeting and finances, cooking, shopping, laundry, form-filling, knowing how to get on housing lists and how to pay for bills. All of these skills and more are also listed as important in the Guidance to the Leaving Care Act.

Aftercare support

Of the 36 young people who had left care, 21 reported receiving some level of aftercare support. Experiences of aftercare support were many and varied and ranged from simply being found a place in a bed-sit at age 16, to receiving quite extensive financial and practical support. One of the more fortunate young people had received a leaving-care grant and help with finding appropriate lodgings, and had had 60 per cent of her student loan covered by her local authority.

It is noteworthy that several young people had not received any support because they had spent little time out of prison since leaving care. In addition, four individuals reported that they had refused the support that was offered to them. Inevitably, some young people will become estranged from their local authority or want nothing more to do with anything that reminds them of their care experience. Some may have returned to live with their birth families or indeed started their own families. However, others may have very little support available to them from elsewhere. It is therefore critical that the local authority makes young people aware that support will still be available to them, up until a certain age, if they choose to accept it at a later date.

On a related note, one criticism made by several care-leavers was that young people are often ill informed about exactly what aftercare support they are entitled to. For example, Jenny (18) noted that you often had to fight for what you wanted.

> There should be support workers, befrienders, all these things should be really accessible for the child. Because my brother's about to leave care as well, and only because he's pushed for…someone to help him along, sort of a befriender person, only because he's pushed for that he's got it. Whereas you know, it's not offered, and a lot of the time kids aren't, can't ask for things like that you know.

As Jenny rightly notes, a lot of the time young people are unable to ask for support or are simply unaware of what support may be available to them.

Amongst those who had received aftercare support in this study, several young people referred to the practical help that they had been given. For example, Ian (17) felt that he had received some useful support. Speaking of his aftercare worker, he commented: 'He has like helped me out with furniture, so I'm seeing him on Tuesday 'cos he's got a wardrobe for me which I desperately need… Plus I've had a leaving-care grant.'

However, others were less positive about the support that they had been provided with. Kate (25), who had been a ward of court from a young age, echoed a theme that emerged earlier regarding Social Services' apparent eagerness to have young people off their hands. After her mother died, Kate did not return to a care placement but instead went to stay with family friends for about a year. This became awkward when the family split up, and Kate was then found a bed-sit by Social Services when she was 15-and-a-half.

> Social Services offered to pay for a bed-sit, at last my freedom. I was working in a nursing home at the time in the kitchens. Social Services came to me to ask if I wanted the wardship to be lifted… Naturally I jumped at the chance. A couple of months after my sixteenth birthday I received a letter from my landlord requesting the rent for the last couple of months. Social Services had stopped paying from my sixteenth birthday and not told me. They had abandoned me.

Similarly, Mark (19) was very much of the opinion that he had had to go it alone soon after his sixteenth birthday, when he was placed in a hostel.

> They placed me in a few hostels and that, and they kind of got fed up in the end 'cos I were kicked out of one of them. Drinking on the premises, taking drugs on the premises and breaking the rules like that and getting caught. I ended up sleeping rough on the streets… They were finding hostels for me and they stuck by me for about two, three, four months. That's it, just told me to go away. Like when I had nowhere to go I would go to the social services department, wait in reception and see me social worker. And reception would just say like 'He doesn't wanna see you, he can do nothing for you', and that was it. So I had to walk out then and find me own way.

Some time after leaving care Mark ended up in prison, as did 13 other young people in this study (recall that a further eight had gone directly from a care placement into custody). Whilst some care-leavers may be really hard work for local authorities to deal with, this does not mean that they should simply 'wash their hands' of young people or, indeed, give up on them. Many individuals leaving care do have problems (some of them as a result of their care experience) but, as corporate parents, surely local authorities have a moral obligation never to turn their back on 16-year-olds with nowhere else to go.

Even those who do have somewhere to go immediately after leaving care will often require a great deal of support. This is particularly so for those who are starting new families and for those who may have brought drug and drink problems with them from care into independent life. Despite some young people's efforts to try to settle down with their own partners upon leaving care, and make the transition to being part of a new family, it is not easy for everyone to keep out of trouble. Drugs and/or alcohol frequently played a part in the stories of those who had been involved in criminal activity after leaving care.

When Jackie (18) found out that she was pregnant, she left care and went to live with her boyfriend and his mother. She had her baby when she was aged 16, but ended up in prison at 18. She associates her offending with a heroin habit that she developed whilst living in residential care.

> I had the baby. Everything was all right for a while, but then I started using heroin again and I got addicted to it and I started getting into trouble, shoplifting, things like that. And then I had to come here 'cos I'd committed crimes.

Similarly, Adele (19) went to live in a flat with her boyfriend after leaving care. Although she had been in prison for a short period when she was aged 15, she described how she had settled down with her boyfriend between the ages of 16 and 17 and kept out of trouble. She then discovered she was pregnant.

> Everything was going fine, but when I got pregnant the baby's dad left me, and I had a drink and I went mad, I went crazy... That's the first time I'd been in trouble since last time I was in here.

Adele was arrested and ended up going back to prison. However, she describes having a baby as a turning point that has changed her outlook on life.

> I'm not into crime any more, I don't agree with it, I've stopped it... That was just one of them mad nights when I was depressed... There's too much to be out for now with the baby and college. I can't wait to get out and get started.

Joe (18) went to jail directly from a care placement. After being released, he moved in with his father. His girlfriend had just had a baby and he started a job in order to make money to support her financially. However, he had a drug problem at the time, and found that he was unable to earn enough to support his habit and support his daughter.

> I wanted to give her more [money] and she [the girlfriend] kept moaning and that and I was having to take drugs to keep awake to get to work... I was having to take drugs to keep awake and everything. In the end I ended up doing a robbery to get money to give to my daughter 'cos I was frightened I'd lose my daughter.

Unfortunately Joe's fears were realised, because he was arrested and later sentenced to a young offender institution for his offences. His daughter was then taken away from his girlfriend and placed in the care system.

The stories of Jackie, Adele and Joe not only serve to highlight the links between drugs, alcohol and offending, but also the fact that just because young people do not have accommodation needs upon leaving care does not mean that they will not require any support at all. Becoming a parent at a young age may be stressful enough in itself, whilst negative coping strategies such as drug and alcohol abuse will often compound the difficulties that vulnerable care-leavers face. It is noteworthy that both Jackie and Adele's drug and alcohol use developed during their time in residential care, although Joe had been using drugs prior to entry to care. Care-leavers who adopt such coping strategies will inevitably need support to address their behaviour (cf. Ward *et al.* 2003).

The need for emotional support

Although several young people in this study reported that they had received varying levels of practical and financial support, very few appeared to have had their emotional needs met. Earlier Beth's story of moving into the 'extension' of the residential home at 16 was outlined. Below she describes what happened when she was required to leave care for good at age 18.

> I was 18, but I don't know. I haven't had a lot of support emotionally all through my life so like I was really really dying for it. I just wanted somebody to be there for me. So I sort of went through a succession of boyfriends…and errm they got me a flat…and I went to live there and I got a leaving-care grant…and then everything went wrong. I got a job and then I got really really depressed so the staff said 'Oh we'll come and see you when we can' but there was just no support, nothing, no consistency again you know. It was like they'd phone up and say 'Oh we'll come next week' and then they'd never turn up…this was the staff from the home. They'd said, you know, 'We'll come and see you' because you know my mum was still drinking and I didn't really want to be with her, 'cos it wasn't helpful and I've no family round here… So basically in the end I got really really depressed, errm tried to jump in the sea, well I did jump in the sea. And I got put in the nut house for depression… I got put in the secure unit, I was sedated and I was in there for about four to five months.

Note Beth's comment 'I just wanted somebody to be there for me'. She was certainly not the only care-leaver to feel this way, and her story illustrates exactly what can happen when young people without support networks become isolated.

Melanie (20) also felt that she was going it alone in her 'supported' lodgings placement.

> And my landlord as well, she didn't care, she was just in it for the money. She had another girl there and it was a case of 'You're not allowed friends in, you're not allowed to use my telephone, you're not allowed to do this, and if you are in after eleven then make sure you're incredibly quiet', and all this… And I ended up sitting in that bedroom for three whole days and not leaving 'cos I just didn't know what to do

with myself. I was just like 'Arrggh, I'm out in the big wide world on my own', and that was when I lost my job. At that point everything started to go really wrong for me.

Whilst Melanie's story raises the question of exactly how 'supported' supported lodgings are supposed to be, what is particularly noteworthy is her final comment – 'at that point everything started to go really wrong for me'. The importance of turning points throughout life, which can help to alter the course of life trajectories (Sampson and Laub 1993), has been emphasised in the theoretical framework underpinning this research. It had been argued that, for some young people, the care experience has the potential to be a positive turning point in their lives. However, the experience of leaving care is also another potential turning point and, sadly, the experiences of many young people indicate that it has often been a negative one.

According to Jenny (18):

I just found that as soon as I hit my eighteenth birthday just no one's wanted to know. My social worker's even said, 'cos I switched social workers just as I moved out of care, and to a lady 'cos the man I had before just didn't understand about counselling and emotional problems. So I asked for a lady and I said to her 'That's what I'm gonna need, a bit more emotional support rather than anything else'. She said 'I can't give that to you, I haven't got the time for that sort of thing', and that was just a real knock-back. I ended up crying my eyes out in front of her.

Under the Children (Leaving Care) Act 2000, it is a statutory requirement that all eligible and relevant young people are appointed a personal adviser. The role of the personal adviser includes providing advice and support and keeping in touch with the young person until he or she is at least 21. The personal adviser has a potentially huge role to play in providing young people with the kind of support that they need. He or she could certainly help to fill the gaps in provision with regard to emotional support that care-leavers in this study identified, and that have been identified elsewhere (Broad 2003).

However, preliminary results from the first national evaluation of the Leaving Care Act (Broad 2003) reveal that, over a year after the Act came into force, only 60 per cent of the 3233 children in the study who were entitled to a personal adviser had one. This left nearly 1300 without one! Given that the appointment of a personal adviser is a statutory requirement these figures are particularly disappointing. They may be explicable in part by a lack of clarity in the legislation concerning who the personal adviser ought to be and, more generally, by the recruitment and retention problems that continue to blight the social care sector.

Social workers and personal advisers

What is evident from the stories above is that some young people leaving care will require a great deal of support, including emotional support. One of the issues discussed with young people in the interviews was what they thought made for a good social worker or key worker. In other words, what qualities did they think a social worker should have? Many individuals had views and opinions on this subject, and although the comments made were in relation to social workers, it may be useful to think about them in relation to personal advisers. The kind of support that young people identified as important whilst in care is perhaps equally important to them once they have left care.

Anne's (18) comment reflected quite a mature understanding of the situation facing many professionals: 'The way of the system is that it is hard for the professionals, there's no doubt about that. It's not *always* their fault, the services aren't always there to provide.' Indeed, although many interviewees had experienced a difficult relationship with a social worker, several young people appeared to appreciate that social work was not always an easy profession to be in.

Anne's criteria for a good social worker were as follows:

> Very much that they have sensitivity of a situation, and they know where to give support and when not to give support maybe. And that they can give good advice, they can be there to support you, to make sure that you make the best decision for you, to guide you along the way.

Meanwhile, Alison (18) noted what was good about her social worker.

> My social worker was lovely, she really was… What was good about her? She actually listened to me, she wouldn't make me do anything if I didn't want to do it, basically just supported me. If I needed a shoulder to cry on she was there.

Whilst acknowledging the difficulties facing child-care professionals, Kate (25) felt that there were still certain things that social workers ought to do.

> There are so many rules and regulations that stop you doing a decent job for the children you are appointed to help. Too many fat cats with budgets, with no idea of what happens in the real world, let alone how children think or feel. But you can be there for the children... Don't make promises you can't keep. Don't make appointments you can't keep, and if you really do have to cancel, speak to the child to make another appointment rather than leaving messages and then not calling for another appointment for ages.

Sadly, the issue of lack of contact with social workers came up time and time again. Helen (18) noted that she had had very little contact after her eighteenth birthday: 'I haven't had contact with my key worker for about three or four months. My social worker's popped into the shop and says she's gonna phone me, but she hasn't. It doesn't bother me in a way.'

Although made in relation to social workers, many of the points above could apply equally well to personal advisers. Young people want someone to help guide them along the way, someone who will listen to them and be there for them if they need a shoulder to cry on. Particularly important is the need to keep in regular contact and not to make promises or appointments that cannot be kept. This latter point is emphasised in Trotter's (1999) discussion of pro-social modelling with involuntary clients. He suggests that workers should model the behaviour that they wish to foster in their client. More recently, Munro (2001) has argued that children interpret their social worker's carelessness over time-keeping and making appointments as a sign of their low priority in the social worker's life. This certainly reflects the comments above made by Kate.

Interestingly, nine interviewees in this study also volunteered that they thought that social workers and/or carers ought to have personal experience that they can draw on, either of the care system or at least of family problems. The role of personal adviser is one that some people with experience of care may be particularly adept at filling – and this is perhaps an avenue that local authorities with a lack of advisers could usefully explore.

Housing issues

One of the major issues facing young people in care is where they will go once they have left care. Under the Leaving Care Act 2000, the duty of local authorities to provide accommodation and maintenance to care-

leavers ends when young people reach 18 (although under the Homelessness Act 2002, care-leavers between 18 and 20 years of age are now
identified as having automatic priority need with regard to housing).
Once care-leavers are 18, local authorities still have a duty to provide
'general assistance' to them up until the age of 21, which includes contributions towards the costs of accommodation.

However, as has been mentioned previously, not only are care placements a scarce resource, but so too is the kind of accommodation available to care-leavers (cf. Barnes and Whitehead 2001; Wade 2003). In
fact, there is a lack of affordable and available accommodation for young
people in the general population. Stein and Wade (2000) recommend
that young people leaving care are offered some choice in the type and
location of accommodation available to them. This is something that
several interviewees in this study would certainly have welcomed.

Helen (18) had no choice at all in where she was placed after leaving
care: 'I didn't like where they dumped me and how they done it. Because
they didn't show me anything, anything else, they kept saying 'Oh the
nearest one's in Oakmead'. But there's got to be some nearer than that.'
Alison (18), who was living with her boyfriend and his relatives at the
time of interview, noted that they had both been offered lodgings by her
aftercare worker. However, this accommodation was so far out of the area
that both she and her boyfriend would have been forced to give up their
full-time jobs: 'She tried putting us in Bridgestead, which means I
couldn't have carried on with my job and he couldn't have carried on
with his job, truly. It just wasn't worth it.'

One way to try and address the problem of the lack of appropriate
accommodation for care-leavers would be to offer more young people
the opportunity to remain in their care placements until 18 and beyond.
What is particularly noteworthy amongst the experiences of young
people in this study is that most individuals in positive foster placements
had the opportunity to stay in foster care until they were 18. For four fortunate young people, their foster placement turned into a supported
lodgings placement on their eighteenth birthday, which enabled individuals to stay on even longer. This allowed them the 'luxury' of experiencing continuity and stability whilst they completed their further education courses.

Whilst such 'staying on' placements can represent a very positive
experience for young people, they have often been dependent on carers
being able to survive financially on a lower allowance. 'Staying on'

placements tend only to be available when young people and carers have developed secure attachment relationships.

Louise (26) emphasised the importance of having a carer who would be prepared to fight your corner. When her older sister Carol was 17, Social Services came round to talk to her about leaving. 'And Lynn said "Don't you dare come round here and tell me she has to leave, she's not ready. And don't you dare come round when Louise is 17 either!"'

Louise eventually left Lynn's when she was 19 and moved in with her fiancé. Carol left when she was aged 21. In complete contrast, the vast majority of those in residential care were required to move on to a new placement when they reached 16, as few of the children's homes that they were in appeared to take individuals after this age. Whilst some children's homes had semi-independence units attached, which enabled individuals to stay on the premises (although this was not always managed helpfully), most young people who had been in residential care were required to move on at 16. The experiences of young people leaving residential placements were incredibly diverse and some were more fortunate than others.

Gail (17) felt that the foyer she had come from before ending up in custody was the best placement she had ever been in. She noted that young people had to be actively looking for work, or else involved in further education, in order to get a place at the foyer.

> You're in your own flat, you get your own bedroom, your own living room and kitchen, your own door keys. You get your gas and electric paid for you but you have to buy your own food... You have to pay a little bit of rent, I think it was about five pounds a week. The only thing that they ask you to comply with is that you're seeing your key worker, your support worker, I think that was once a week, and that you didn't take drugs on the premises.

Stein (1997) notes that the foyer initiative in the UK, based on the French system of 'Foyer des Jeunes Travailleurs', developed as a response to the dual problem of homelessness and unemployment amongst young people rather than for care-leavers in particular. However, Gail's story above indicates that the foyers may well be very useful to care-leavers. Based on the principle of social inclusion, the foyer initiative seeks to improve young people's chances of gaining employment and finding more permanent housing.

Interestingly, Vernon (2000) points out that the foyer initiative remains a relatively new and untested idea in the UK. In her audit and assessment of leaving-care services in London, she found that most social services departments 'expressed considerable scepticism about their appropriateness for other than a very small group of care-leavers' (p.77). However, in comparison to some of the other options available, those placed in a foyer in this study seemed to be relatively fortunate. If foyers are as new and untested as Vernon suggests, then their merits certainly ought to be explored further by local authorities.

Inappropriate accommodation

At the other end of the scale, a significant number of young people were placed in hostels and bed-sits where they received very little support. This kind of accommodation is clearly inappropriate for the majority of care-leavers, yet ironically it tended to be provided for the youngest care-leavers in this study. The experience of being in a bed-sit or hostel seemed to be made worse for many individuals by the behaviour of other residents.

Kate (25) was placed in a bed-sit when she was 15-and-a-half.

> At my bedsit I was having awful problems with an alcoholic man, he even tried to break into my room sometimes with a hammer. He would terrorise the whole house, keeping us awake all night. Some of the other residents would hide in my room.

Michael (18) first went into a hostel at age 16.

> And they were all old men and mad women and that. They were all like 60-odd…there was a couple of young ones, but it was just weird, you know what I mean… And there was a probation hostel opposite with all like sex offenders and all that in as well. It wasn't good living there.

Donnie (19) did not enjoy being in a hostel either:

> (Y)ou get put in these hostels and they're full of [*pause*] smackheads is my word, smackheads. They were drugged and with needles and that. And I don't like that, you sit there and you look at them and you can tell what they're on.

One would like to think that the kind of accommodation described above would be used as a last resort for vulnerable young care-leavers. However, such is the lack of accommodation available for care-leavers and the young homeless in general that this kind of provision seems to be increasingly used. In London, Vernon (2000) found that many boroughs had been using direct-access hostels as emergency accommodation, and when these were full, placements sometimes had to be made in bed and breakfast (B&B) accommodation.

Certain young people in this study also reported having been placed in B&B accommodation and occasionally in hotels on a short-term basis. The shortage of affordable accommodation up and down the country does not look set to change in the immediate future. Furthermore, the recent influx of asylum seekers and unaccompanied children to Britain is placing additional demands on a housing service that already appears to be stretched to the limit. (It is noteworthy that unaccompanied asylum-seeking children are covered by the provisions in the Leaving Care Act, although they will also have an immigration status that local authorities need to take account of.)

Under the Homelessness Act 2002, local housing authorities are now required to formulate a homelessness strategy and to consider how to secure accommodation for those who are homeless or at risk of home-lessness. This ought to highlight specific problems and local housing needs in different areas of the country. However, the lack of accommoda-tion currently available to care-leavers is an enduring problem and will certainly place difficulties upon local authorities trying to fulfil their new duties to young people who have been in care (cf. Ward 2003). Whilst some young people have the option to return to their birth families once they have left care, this is not the case for everyone and many will need to establish a base of their own.

In this study the majority of young people in positive foster place-ments were able to stay in care until they were at least 18. Yet this was not the case for those leaving residential placements, who were generally required to move on at 16. Some of these young people were placed in hostels and bed-sits, the more fortunate individuals in foyers and well-supported lodgings. Amongst those in supported lodgings and semi-independence units, many were required to move on again at the age of 18. The important point is that while young people in foster care may be able to stay in their placements up to the age of 18 and beyond, those in residential care are often more likely to begin making the transi-tion to independence at 16 as few have the opportunity to remain in the same placement after this time. It therefore appears that young people leaving residential care may be much more vulnerable to the difficulties associated with independent living at an early age.

From care to custody

Given that young people leaving care continue to make the transition to independence at a much earlier age than their peers, are often inadequately prepared for coping alone and are frequently placed in inappropriate accommodation with very little support, it is not so surprising that a disproportionate number of care-leavers end up in the prison population.

Research by the Home Office based on focus groups with young offenders found that many had spent long periods of time in the care system (Lyon *et al.* 2000). The comments made by the young people reiterate some of the themes discussed in this chapter.

> They described how their need for help in facing the transition from care to independence went unmet. The particular difficulties they described facing were around housing, sources of income and managing finances... Crime was seen as a response to the need to gain money and materials for survival after being let down by the care system. (pp.12–13)

In this study five young people (all of whom were male) reported having slept rough on the streets after leaving care. This was not something that interviewees were specifically asked about. However, given the experiences described by many after leaving care, it is quite possible that this figure would have been higher had everyone been asked a direct question about it. Rough sleeping is often another stepping stone into custody, since young people tend to commit crimes as a means of survival.

Donnie (19) left care at 16 and was placed in a flat.

> They got me a flat what was sixty quid a week to pay, and I was on a training scheme which paid me fifty quid a week. And I don't know how I was meant to, and the housing benefit weren't, you know sometimes it mixes up doesn't it, they weren't paying me. So I basically ended up on the street and I just sacked the training scheme... I've just gone downhill ever since then... I'm 19 now, I've been coming to prison since...like what 16 or something, 17. Not very nice really.

Although Donnie notes that coming to prison is 'not very nice', recall that in Chapter 5 he compared it to being in care: 'It used to be like care if you know what I mean when I first started coming to jail. It used to be like "yeah, I'm back in care" kind of thing.' Attachment to an institutional way of life was also referred to by Jackie, but in reference to her young offender institution. In her words: 'If I didn't have me son, or anything like that, and if I didn't have a place to live, then you know it would be the next place to home really for me.' Meanwhile, in Chapter 6, Gemma noted that it was very easy to get used to life in prison, 'because everyone I knew was in here, from the kids' homes. It was like a big family reunion!'

When we consider some of the difficulties facing many young people leaving care, is it any wonder that they find comfort in an institutional setting such as prison? Perhaps a sense of comfort also comes from recognising so many other young people from similar backgrounds. At the age of 18, Michael had been placed in custody five times since leaving care at 16.

> Like I've been here for 13 months and I'm just used to it, institutionalised. It's just the norm, it's everyday. In the last three years I've only been out about four weeks or something. Like the last time I got out I was out for four days before I got arrested for something else. Like what kind of life's that? Four days and then back in.

Yet leaving jail was clearly a worrying prospect for Michael.

> Michael: I worry more about getting out than I do about coming in… Because when you get out you're getting out and you haven't even got nowhere to live, you know what I mean? 'Cos I can't go and stay with me mum or dad, so then I've got to go to a hostel and wait in there on a council waiting list. And then I've got to wait for a flat, and it takes whatever, however long. And once you've got your flat you've gotta find the money to like decorate it, buy furniture and like all the things you need and all that. You get grants but like it's not enough. And then you've got to start to think about ways to get money. Do you know what I mean, that's before you've even got out, you're thinking of ways of how to get money.
>
> Claire: You mean like nicking money?
>
> Michael: Yeah.

Similarly, Kane (19) noted that some young people wanted to come back to jail.

> Kane: A lot of people in here they wanna do long stretches... A lad's just got out but he loves jail, he loves coming to jail. He thinks it's brilliant.
>
> Claire: Why does he think that?
>
> Kane: It's just like, people live like tramps and things on the out. They come to jail yeah, they get three meals a day, a bed and you've got tellies and things now... You don't have to sleep under a bus stop or whatever, it's like this is better than that...I don't have to worry about where I'm gonna eat next or anything like that.

In many ways, the fact that some young people want to return to jail, and others worry more about getting out than they do about coming in, is a damning indictment of the support available to them after leaving care. It is a very sad finding that some young people have been so inadequately prepared for life in the real world that they do not want to have to cope on their own (cf. Carlen 1987).

Liz (17) noted in relation to the prison where she was:

> It's just like a home, people get used to it and they think they need to go back. And they go out there and they think they just can't cope, because we get everything in here, do you know what I mean? We get our food and everything... Like you've got no sense of independence in here, and when you're doing a long sentence it's hard out there, I can see it being hard for me.

Eligible and relevant children continue to qualify for the duties in the Leaving Care Act 2000, even if they are sentenced to prison or serving a community sentence. As is documented in the Regulations and Guidance covering the Act, 'they may be in particular need of help from their responsible authority' (DH 2001c, p.22). What the stories above highlight is that it is absolutely crucial that care-leavers in prison are made aware that there will actually be support out there for them.

As I have argued elsewhere (Taylor 2003), care-leavers who regard prison as a home from home have not made a successful transition to independence and, in this sense, have been failed by their local authorities. These young people in particular may need a great deal of support when they return to the community. On an encouraging note, Broad (2003) has recently identified 'some improvement' to leaving-care services for young people post-custody since the Leaving Care Act came into force. However, he emphasises the need for this often-neglected group to receive higher priority and further investment in the future.

Summary

The leaving-care experiences of young people in this study were generally poor, regardless of whether or not individuals had had a positive experience whilst in the care system. Four young people were able to stay with their foster carers beyond the age of 18 when these placements turned into supported lodgings. It has been suggested that enabling young people to stay with their carers up until 18 and beyond may provide them with some much-needed stability and continuity. Unfortunately, few local authorities enable young people to stay in their placements, even when they are settled and wish to stay (Stein 1997).

Amongst the rest of the interviewees, those in foster placements generally had the opportunity to stay on until they reached 18, whilst those in residential care usually had to begin making the transition from care to independence at 16. Young people leaving care were placed in a diverse range of accommodation, ranging from well-supported foyers and semi-independence units to entirely inappropriate bed-sits and hostels. Thirteen young people went on to serve a custodial sentence after leaving care and a further eight moved directly from a care placement into custody. Those who had problems with drugs and alcohol after leaving care seemed particularly at risk of involvement in crime.

One question running throughout the chapter has been how far the Children (Leaving Care) Act 2000 is relevant to the experiences of young people in this study. If implemented properly, can it fill the gaps in provision that have been identified in this chapter? A straight answer to that is that it could certainly help. Many of the issues that care-leavers in this study regarded as important, such as adequate preparation for independence, are also highlighted as important in the Guidance to the new legislation. However, translating the legislation into effective practice could well prove to be a challenge.

Effective implementation of the Leaving Care Act may be problematic for a number of reasons. First, the shortage of carers in the country means that social workers continue to be under pressure to free up placements and those approaching leaving-care age rarely have the option to stay on. Second, the shortage of staff in the social care sector more generally may mean that personal advisers are not always there to provide for every child. Another major concern is that suitable accommodation for young people who are leaving care is a seriously scarce resource. In order for local authorities to fulfil their duty of providing accommodation to all eligible and relevant 16- and 17-year-olds, it is crucial that more appropriate lodgings are made available.

Finally, one of the weaknesses of the new legislation is that it does not go far enough in the provision it offers to care-leavers. The duty upon local authorities to provide accommodation ends when young people reach 18 (although 18- to 20-year-old care-leavers will have automatic housing priority need under the Homelessness Act 2002). Therefore, some individuals will presumably be moving out of care just as they are trying to finish their A-levels or other further education courses. For many young people in care, the approach of their eighteenth birthday will continue to be a dreaded date.

Leaving care at 18 is not appropriate for everyone, and some young people may require more support than others. Local authorities still have duties to provide 18- to 21-year-olds with general assistance and financial support, and it is very important that they do provide these individuals with the help that they need. Better support is not only necessary for young people's welfare needs and rights, but also as a crime prevention measure. If not provided with adequate and appropriate after-care support, care-leavers are far more likely to reappear in the criminal justice system or the mental health system at a later date. On a more positive note, early indications suggest that the Children (Leaving Care) Act 2000 has led to some progress, albeit uneven, in leaving-care services (Broad 2003). The challenge for the future is to ensure that this progress is extended and maintained.

Part III
Conclusion

Chapter 8

Key findings and implications for policy and practice

Introduction

Since I embarked upon the project described in this book, a great deal of government attention has been directed at the local authority care system. One result of this has been the introduction of a wealth of new legislation and policy initiatives relating to young people in care. Consequently it has been a very interesting time to be studying the care system. For example, in the year 2000 official statistics were published for the first time on the educational qualifications of care-leavers. In the same year, a new statistical collection was introduced that considered the offending rates of looked-after children. It is quite remarkable that the state care system has never before been required to measure such results (a further indicator of the very low priority traditionally afforded to the care system). However, the official knowledge base that is currently being constructed is an important step forward.

This study has attempted to engage with the rapidly changing policy climate and relevant new legislation and research. The important point for the purposes of the current discussion is that in between the formulation of the research questions and completion of the study presented here, the situation facing young people in and leaving care has shifted. In this final chapter I outline the key findings from my research and explain how the implications of these findings led me to conclude that things need to shift much further. Recommendations for policy and practice are made, and there is a discussion of future priorities for research in this area. It is of course unlikely that government interest in young people in care will be sustained indefinitely. Indeed, the momentum of the Quality Protects machine may not last much longer as the programme is due to finish in the near future. Therefore, with regard to policy recommendations in particular, it is clear that the time for change is now.

Key findings
The diversity of care experiences

One of the first things to become immediately clear in this project was that there is a very diverse range of care experiences. The backgrounds that young people came from, and the experiences of family life that they brought with them into care, were many and varied. Amongst those interviewed, some had chosen to go into care themselves; others were placed by the courts and some by their families. Certain individuals experienced just foster or residential care placements, but many had experienced both. A small number of interviewees went into care at ages as young as three years, others as late as 16 or 17.

Some young people spent a great deal of time moving back and forth between different care placements and their own homes. Others never returned home after an admission to care had taken place. Some individuals welcomed going into care, others hated the fact that they were in care, and others still felt that as it was the only life that they had ever known, they could not really compare it to anything else.

The key point is that popular perceptions that lump all young people in care together are very misleading and ignore the various different routes that individuals may take through the care system. As I have argued elsewhere (e.g. Taylor 2004), the common labelling of children in care as 'mad' or 'bad' stems from a failure to appreciate the diverse range of care experiences that actually exist. This lack of understanding is not only reflected in public assumptions about the care system, but also in policy and practice. A common complaint to emerge about Social Services was the lack of individualised care provided, and the fact that young people are often treated the same regardless of their needs. As one individual commented: 'I didn't feel it was personalised for me enough. I kept thinking I've been through different things from all the other kids I've met. Why am I being treated the same?'

Mayhem in residential care

Despite the great diversity in individual care careers, there were inevitably some recurrent themes in the experiences that young people described. Some common findings emerged in relation to particular types of care provision. With regard to life in residential care, many interviewees painted an incredibly bleak and depressing picture. It is important to note that some positive experiences of children's homes did exist and that foster care was not appropriate for everyone (also, some young people went to children's homes because of foster placement breakdowns). However, in this study, positive experiences were few and far between when compared to the mayhem and misery experienced by many young people in a residential setting.

Stories of life in residential care often made reference to bullying, self-harming, uncontrollable children running wild and a perceived couldn't-care-less attitude on the part of disillusioned staff. To repeat the words of one young woman: 'You're not encouraged to move on when you're in a home, you just exist, that's it. You're still breathing, you've been fed, you've got clothes on your back, that's it.' Such findings seem to have resonance with Colton's (2002) recent assertion that the residential child-care sector in the UK is a national disgrace.

One particularly noteworthy finding in this study was the prevalence of offending behaviour by residents. Twenty-three young people spoke of getting into trouble during their stay in a residential setting; 11 of these claimed to have been in trouble with the police for criminal offences prior to being admitted to care. For those who had already been involved in offending, going into care seemed to have little effect in crime prevention terms. For many young men in particular, their criminal behaviour appeared to escalate.

It could be argued that the 11 individuals who had previously been in trouble with the police simply followed their criminal career trajectory once in the care system. This view lends support for self-control theory (Gottfredson and Hirschi 1990) and the related argument that an individual's propensity for crime is set in early childhood and remains relatively stable throughout life. However, self-control theory cannot adequately explain why an additional 12 young people in this study, who had not previously been in trouble with the police, starting getting into trouble once in the care system. Some of these individuals did not go into care until their early to mid-teens, a long time after the age of eight when low self-control is supposed to become established (cf. Gottfredson and Hirschi 1990).

Whilst there were various reasons that young people put forward for their involvement in crime, a striking theme to emerge in many of the stories told was that there was always a crowd to follow. In other words, a deviant subculture often already existed in the residential homes, which resulted in some new residents being introduced to delinquency. The experiences of many of the young people interviewed confirm that institutionalised adolescents continue to be heavily influenced by their peers (cf. Polsky 1962).

Criminal careers can lead to care careers, as we know; for example, through young people being remanded into care. However, the findings in this study highlight that the relationship also works the other way round. Certain types of care career, particularly those associated with some of the worst features of life in a residential setting, can intensify, create and promote criminal behaviour (Taylor 2004).

Having someone who cares

In addition, certain types of care experience, particularly those associated with stability, security and a quality relationship with carers, can help to protect against involvement in crime. Having someone who cares emerged as a highly significant theme in this respect. Amongst those interviewees who had been involved in crime, many spoke of feeling that nobody cared about them once they were placed in care. They therefore felt that they had nobody to be bothered about and were free to behave as they wished. This was a particularly common finding amongst those who had been in residential care, where a lack of staff continuity frequently contributed to residents feeling that nobody really knew what was happening in their lives.

Foster care, on the other hand, seemed to offer more potential for carers and young people to get to know one another, and ten individuals were identified as having developed secure attachments with their foster carers. These relationships tended to develop in the context of long-term foster placements (although placements were not always initially intended to be long term). The stories of those who had developed secure attachments in the context of care highlighted the crucial importance of being sensitive to the opinion of others (Hirschi 1969). They also highlighted that it is possible for young people to develop secure relationships with their carers, even after being placed at a relatively late age (cf. Downes 1992; Schofield 2003).

Having respect for a carer and not wanting to let him or her down were identified as important aspects of the care experience that could protect against involvement in crime or prevent further offending. Furthermore, those who had developed meaningful relationships with their carers were far more likely to reflect upon their care experience in positive terms and to have a positive self-image. Developing secure attachments to carers can enable resilience to previous psychosocial adversity. However, in order for such relationships to develop, certain care conditions need to be in place. For example, young people must experience care as a secure and stable base. The experiences of those who had developed secure attachments highlighted that, contrary to common assumptions, some care experiences can in fact be very positive.

Promoting self-esteem through education

Interestingly, as the case of one young man demonstrated, the attachment relationship alone may not necessarily be enough to protect against involvement in crime. Put simply, it is not always enough to have someone who cares about you and believes in you. In addition to this, you need to care about yourself and believe in yourself too. It may be that the former acts as a catalyst for the latter. However, both are important. Involvement in school life and a commitment to education have been highlighted as particularly important factors that can promote self-esteem and self-belief. Such involvement and commitment are often intrinsically related to secure attachments with carers in protecting young people from involvement in crime.

However, as with the development of supportive relationships with carers, involvement in education tends to be reliant on young people experiencing some degree of stability in their lives. Constant movement within the care system and constant movement in and out of the care system often result in school changes and confound the likelihood that young people will experience stability and security in the context of care.

The experiences of many young people in this study serve to reinforce the well-established link between low educational attainment and offending behaviour, and low educational attainment and experience of care. However, a small number of individuals had obtained some of the highest grades at school and at college. It is important to acknowledge that many young people have difficulties with school, or have missed large chunks of their schooling, prior to their entry to care. Finding a stable placement can improve this situation and indeed did so for several young people. Yet often the care system appeared to create more problems than it solved. The low priority afforded to education by some residential carers was a particularly disturbing finding in this respect.

Care careers that are characterised by constant movement between placements and between schools, and which neither emphasise the value of education nor provide young people with support and encouragement in their learning, can intensify educational failure in some cases and create it in others. By contrast, care careers that are characterised by stability, and supportive relationships with carers who take an active interest in young people's progress and development, can help to improve educational attainment.

Leaving care as a turning point

Leaving care is an important turning point for most young people, which signals that their care career is coming to an end. How the leaving-care process is managed can have a significant effect on what happens to individuals after care. With regard to improving outcomes for care-leavers in general, and reducing offending behaviour in particular, it is as important to pay attention to the leaving-care process as it is to focus on young people's experiences whilst in the care system.

Regardless of whether or not individuals had had a positive experience whilst in care, the leaving-care experiences described in this study were generally poor. Several young people felt that their local authorities had abandoned them and most interviewees felt that they had been inadequately prepared for independent living. Those in foster placements were more likely to have the chance to stay on in care until they were aged 18 (with a lucky few staying even longer), whilst those leaving residential placements tended to begin making the transition to independence when they were 16.

Several of the stories told highlighted how easy it is for young people without any support networks to become isolated after care. Isolation can lead to depression and again the feeling that nobody cares. Sometimes drugs and/or alcohol will be used as coping strategies, which, in turn, may contribute to offending behaviour. It was noticeable that those who had problems with drugs and alcohol after leaving care were particularly at risk of involvement in crime. In order to help prevent such outcomes, it is absolutely crucial that care-leavers receive the support and help that they need. It is noteworthy that those who were involved in further education, and who remained in contact with carers to whom they had developed secure attachments, were less likely to offend or become isolated after care.

The young people in this study were of course describing experiences that took place prior to the implementation of the Children (Leaving Care) Act 2000. The gloomy experiences of many interviewees ought to be set against the concerted efforts in recent years to improve the situation for care-leavers. New legislation has the potential to make leaving care a much more positive experience for young people than it has been in the past. However, an analysis of the current policy climate has revealed that there are some serious inconsistencies in New Labour's approach to helping young people in care. In particular, some of the positive welfare-based initiatives that have been introduced by the government have the potential to be undermined by the more punitive aspects of youth justice policy. This may well have grave consequences for young people in care who break the law.

Recommendations for policy and practice

On the basis of the findings outlined above, there are various recommendations to be made that are relevant to policy and practice. Although the government has demonstrated a commitment to improving the public care system, and the experiences of young people within it, there is much work still to do.

Promote individuality, challenge popular perceptions and raise expectations

First, this study has emphasised the need to respond to looked-after children and care-leavers as individuals. This requires recognition of both the diverse range of experiences that young people in care bring with them and the variety of different pathways that they may take through the care system. Recognising and promoting the individuality of young people in care requires understanding their cases in some depth. It also involves appreciating that what is appropriate for one person may not be appropriate for everyone. Practitioners and carers need to take a flexible approach in order to ensure that individual needs are fully met. Young people do not want to be viewed or treated as the 'children's home kids' or 'care kids', but as individuals in their own right (Taylor 2004).

Furthermore, there is a need to challenge popular perceptions that routinely link children in care with trouble. The negative labelling commonly associated with being in care is not only stigmatising but also contributes directly to low expectations. Low expectations are associated with poor outcomes and often fuel dangerous and narrow-minded assumptions about individuals in care (cf. Birch and Taylor 2003). Promoting the notion of resilience (Gilligan 2001) is one important way forward in terms of raising expectations of children looked after by the state.

Recognise the importance of foster and residential care provision

This study should definitely not be interpreted as a residential care versus foster care debate. The particular themes focused on happen to have resulted in an emphasis on some of the best aspects of foster care and the worst aspects of residential care. However, one thing that is evident from the findings in this study is that we need both types of provision. Although residential provision is frequently regarded as the poor relation of foster care, both need to be regarded as a positive option. The 'last resort' mentality associated with residential care must be replaced with more ambitious aims and objectives for residents and carers so that both groups are valued.

Improve the residential care experience

The stories of young people in this study support the view that residential care experiences may be enhanced when units are smaller. Smaller units can provide more individualised care for children and may reduce the likelihood of some residents developing and maintaining a deviant sub-culture. The power of peer pressure is also likely to be reduced when there are fewer peers to pressurise.

Furthermore, policy-makers and practitioners should aim to promote staff continuity in the residential sector. This may be a more realistic goal in smaller homes, where fewer residents would result in fewer staff. It is incredibly difficult for young people to get to know their carers, and indeed feel that they have someone to talk to, when staff are constantly coming and going. However, if a smaller staff group worked more regularly in the same unit, there may be more opportunities for staff and young people to at least get to know one another and potentially establish some trust and respect. Young people in care need to have someone to whom they can turn, and the importance of feeling that someone actually cares cannot be emphasised enough.

On a related note, residential care staff need to be aware to look out for the signs of self-harming; they should also be trained in how to approach this issue with residents who self-harm. As with offending behaviour, self-harming should not be allowed to become just another element of day-to-day living in residential care. Staff and social workers must help and encourage young people to address the reasons behind such behaviour. For residents who are persistently involved in offending, specific attention to criminal attitudes and behaviour may also be needed.

Finally, one key challenge for the residential sector in the future is to avoid a situation where some young people actually prefer being in prison to being in a children's home. Certain individuals in this study noted that they felt safer and more secure in a prison environment than they had done in their previous residential placement, and this is very worrying. In particular, the comments regarding prison officers being far more bothered than residential carers about young people's well-being are a damning indictment of the care provided in the residential sector. In this respect, the government's aim of 'making sure that child care workers are fit for the job' (DH 1999, p.4) is an extremely important goal to pursue.

Prevent the unnecessary criminalisation of looked-after children

Evidence from interviewees in this study and research from elsewhere (NACRO 2003b) suggest that young people in children's homes may be more likely to be prosecuted for relatively minor offences such as criminal damage in the home. One consequence is that looked-after children may find themselves introduced to the criminal justice system at an early age for behaviour that would not necessarily result in an official intervention if they were living at home with their parents. The routine prosecution of minor offences in some children's homes is likely to be a significant barrier to reducing the offending rates of children in care. More worryingly, it can contribute to these children being unnecessarily criminalised.

There is a serious need for local authorities to address this problem. NACRO (2003b) recently found that some local authorities have implemented protocols between Social Services and the police, setting out guidelines for residential staff on how best to respond to disruptive behaviour. The guidelines encourage staff to question when it is actually appropriate to respond to an incident by calling the police, and have the potential to significantly reduce the number of children being unnecessarily prosecuted. Local authorities that have not yet done so could usefully take steps to begin implementing such a protocol in their area; in the first instance, for example, by initiating a meeting between the local police and children's home managers.

Keep placement changes to a minimum

The findings in this study support the well-established recommendation that placement changes should be kept to a minimum in order to provide young people with some degree of stability and continuity in their lives. In addition, this study provides support for Minty's (1999) claim that the current policy of short-term admissions to care may not always be in the child's best interests. This is because it can encourage the 'oscillation' of children in and out of care, with the result that some long-term admissions are simply postponed.

The experiences of young people in this study confirm that, other than when some form of short-term respite care is provided, the policy of placing individuals in and out of care is rarely helpful. It frequently results in young people failing to experience a stable base either inside or outside of the care system, and it should be avoided where possible. By contrast, the potentially positive benefits of long-term foster care ought to have more recognition (Schofield 2003). Although long-term foster care is not appropriate for everyone, the findings in this study suggest that it provides the most realistic opportunity for young people to develop secure attachments with their carers.

Encourage young people to achieve their potential

When young people experience stability and continuity in their lives, it is also more likely that they will be able to benefit from involvement in school life and education. Emphasising the value of education to young people in care is of crucial importance, particularly as achievement at school can have such a positive impact on self-esteem. Unfortunately, education has traditionally been afforded a very low priority in the care system. It is horrifying to discover that for some care-leavers it is only when they end up studying for courses in prison that they realise that they are actually capable of achieving educationally.

We need to be much more ambitious for young people in the care system, and it is the duty of teachers and carers to encourage and support individuals in their learning. A recent report by the Social Exclusion Unit (SEU 2003) outlines some valuable ways to move forward on this issue. For example, raising expectations of young people in care amongst teachers, carers and social workers is identified as one of the key ways to promote educational attainment. The report also highlights the importance of rewarding young people's achievements. It is important to note that there are now some encouraging signs that attitudes are changing and more resources are being allocated to the education of children in care. However, considerable commitment is needed to ensure that this progress is maintained (Jackson and Sachdev 2001).

Provide aftercare support appropriate to individual needs

One of the ironic things about the care system is that although we expect less of young people who are in care, in terms of educational attainment for example, we expect more of care-leavers than their peers in terms of independent living. Under the Children (Leaving Care) Act 2000, care-leavers will continue to experience accelerated and compressed transitions to adulthood in comparison to their peers. However, if implemented properly, this new legislation certainly has the potential to make leaving care a much more supported and positive experience than it has been in the past. The stories in this study indicate how important it is that individuals receive aftercare support that is appropriate to their needs.

Furthermore, there is a need for local authorities to enable more young people to stay in their care placements beyond the age of 18. Foster placements that turn into supported lodgings when a young person reaches 18 are particularly valuable in this respect. Once young people have left the care system, however, there seems to be a shortage of appropriate accommodation in which they can be housed. The lack of affordable and available provision for care-leavers is a structural problem that could be a barrier to the successful implementation of the new Leaving Care Act. This is something that local authorities need to address and, indeed, the new Homelessness Act 2002 requires them to do so.

With regard to young people who receive a custodial sentence, it is crucial that procedures are in place to ensure effective throughcare planning and support (NACRO 2003b). (Such procedures can be linked in to local authority care plans and reviews for looked-after children on a care order.) There is a need for social workers to consider the action that is required to keep in touch with the young person while he or she is in custody. For example, does the young person have a mentor or personal adviser to support him or her? Are those eligible for the provisions under the Children (Leaving Care) Act aware of what support will be available to them? What sort of help is available for those children who do not fulfil the Act's criteria for eligibility? Planning for return to the community must begin at an early stage and in consultation with the young person (Taylor 2003).

Review and join up policy

Looked-after children and care-leavers who do get into trouble with the police may be in particular need of help from their local authority. However, they may also be subject to various punitive youth justice measures. The disjointed policy assumptions relating to young offenders and children in need represent a real barrier to reducing the offending rates of looked-after children and to improving their life chances more generally. Whilst the government has demonstrated a commitment to protecting vulnerable children, it has failed to place the welfare of children at the heart of the youth justice system, despite widespread condemnation of the way we treat children in trouble.

Youth justice policies should be urgently reviewed and joined up with the welfare-based policies relating to young people in care. This is particularly important for youth justice measures that treat children in trouble primarily as offenders rather than as children in need (cf. Goldson 2002a). Many young people who come into contact with the justice system have also been in the care system. For these vulnerable individuals, a harsh and punitive response to their offending behaviour is highly unlikely to be helpful.

Interestingly, although policy-makers often travel to continental Europe and North America in search of answers to the 'crime problem', it may be that there is more to be learnt from closer to home. A welfare-based approach to youth justice, which prioritises the welfare of children in trouble, has endured for over 30 years in Scotland with no apparent rise in the crime rate (Smith 2000). Whilst the Scottish youth justice system is not perfect and has been criticised, it does demonstrate the feasibility of a welfare-based approach to dealing with children who break the law. Policy-makers in the field of youth justice in England and Wales could usefully learn from some of the principles underpinning both the Scottish system and the care system.

Greater dialogue between child care and criminology

The current detachment of policies within the care and criminal justice systems is also reflected at the theoretical level in the fields of child care and criminology, where theoretical insights have tended to remain within the disciplinary borders from whence they came. It has been argued that insights from criminological theory provide a useful wider frame of reference for research on the care system, and specifically research on the link between care and crime. The key concept of attachment offers a useful starting point for attempting to make connections between the two areas of study. Both have drawn on ideas about attachment, but used and interpreted these ideas in different ways. There is value in bringing together the two literatures.

Adopting a relational life-course approach to care may offer researchers and practitioners some fresh ideas with which to approach their work. Of particular importance is that such a framework not only has space for optimism, but positively encourages it. Following Sampson and Laub (1993), a criminological life-course approach recognises the relative stability of certain individual traits, whilst acknowledging that turning points throughout life can redirect pathways.

If managed helpfully, experiences of care and leaving care could both be potentially positive turning points in young people's lives. With this in mind, productive links could also be made between the notion of resilience (Gilligan 2001) in child welfare and the notion of desistance (see Maruna 2001) in criminology. Whilst taking account of what has occurred in the past, both emphasise the capacity of individuals to live positive, productive lives in the future. Regardless of early negative experiences, outcomes in adulthood are not necessarily set in stone and there are a variety of pathways that individuals may take through life. Therefore, child-care professionals should regard themselves as active agents in helping to determine young people's futures.

Future priorities

In light of the research presented in this book, there are various ways forward to further explore the complex interaction between care and criminal careers. First, one key question that would be well worth investigating is whether males are able to develop, and benefit from, quality attachments with substitute carers in the same way as females. Recent work in criminology suggests that males are particularly vulnerable to the effects of early attachment disruptions, and that this accounts for high male crime rates (Hayslett-McCall and Bernard 2002). Whilst the gender balance of young people in this study has not allowed for an examination of this topic, future research could usefully explore this issue in some depth.

Whilst it is very important to ensure that the voices of young people with first-hand experience of the care system continue to be heard, it would be helpful for future research to combine these voices with more quantitative details about the offending of looked-after children. If it were possible to access personal files and official criminal records, there could be scope for creating a database to show the numbers of young people coming into contact with the police prior to their entry to care, during their time in care and after they have left the care system. This kind of information may enable the development of a typology of offenders with experience of care.

In addition, there is a need to consider how inter-agency cooperation between child-care and youth offending teams could help to improve outcomes for young people in the care system. What might be the most efficient way for these agencies to share information so that looked-after children who offend do not become lost in the criminal justice system? Ensuring that youth justice workers are aware of the 'looked-after' status of relevant young offenders could certainly help to highlight the vulnerability of these individuals.

One way forward, in terms of information sharing, may be for Social Services, youth offending teams and others to become familiar with the working arrangements and assessment tools used by those working in neighbouring fields (Hagell 2003). This would draw the attention of individual agencies to data that might be available to them from elsewhere and to information that could be shared rather than duplicated. Recent evidence also suggests that providing opportunities for staff from youth offending teams and looked-after children's services to train alongside each other can help local authorities to reduce the offending rates of children in care. NACRO (2003b) found that this encouraged the joint ownership of a commitment to prevent young people offending.

With regard to policy analysis, an evaluation of the impact of the Children (Leaving Care) Act 2000 will clearly be a future priority. In particular, there will be a need to consider whether local authorities have sufficient resources to fully implement the provisions of the Act. Preliminary findings offer a mixed picture on the impact of the Leaving Care Act over a year after it came into force, although it is clear that progress has been made in certain areas (Broad 2003). However, a major challenge for the future is to ensure that progress is extended and maintained. The majority of government funding provided so far has been ring-fenced. However, as Broad suggests, local authorities will need ongoing and additional funds to ensure that services for care-leavers do not return to their inadequate pre-2000 service levels.

Finally, with regard to future priorities, there is a need to consider the implications of a potentially changing care population over the next few years. Conflict on a global scale has resulted in an increasing number of asylum seekers and displaced persons fleeing from their home countries. The arrival of unaccompanied children to Britain is placing heavy demands on social services departments in certain parts of the UK. Furthermore, recent government proposals for an intensive fostering service to be developed with respect to persistent young offenders are likely to have additional resource implications. It is important to consider how the specific needs of all these individuals can be met. What kinds of specialist support will they require, and what new resources will be required to meet their needs? These questions represent new and ongoing challenges to local authorities trying to fulfil their duties to young people in the care system.

Concluding thoughts

The research presented in this book has used the voices of young people who have been in care to illuminate various aspects of the care experience. It has been argued that certain types of care experience can create and promote offending behaviour. In such instances, local authorities have failed in their duty as corporate parents to provide young people with the care and support that they need. In the current policy climate there is a danger that looked-after children who offend will be failed even further when they come into contact with a punitive youth justice system. Policies that punish and exclude, without any supportive interventions, will only serve to ensure that future generations of care-leavers continue to be over-represented in the prison population.

On a more optimistic note, this study has demonstrated that certain types of care experience can be very positive for some young people and can help to protect against involvement in crime. We need to be much more ambitious for looked-after children, and there is much to be learnt from the stories of those who feel that care has had a positive impact on their lives. The very existence of these individuals means that there is absolutely no reason to assume that looked-after children will inevitably and obviously fare worse and achieve less than other young people.

References

Ainsworth, M.D., Blehar, M.C., Waters, E. and Wall, S. (1978) *Patterns of Attachment.* New Jersey: Erlbaum.

Barnes, V. and Whitehead, K. (2001) *An Evaluation of Coventry Aftercare Project: A Report for NCH Action for Children.* Coventry: Coventry University.

Berridge, D. (1997) *Foster Care: A Research Review.* London: The Stationery Office.

Berridge, D. and Brodie, I. (1998) *Children's Homes Revisited.* London: Jessica Kingsley Publishers.

Biehal, N. and Wade, J. (1999) '"I thought it would be easier": The early housing careers of young people leaving care.' In J. Rugg (ed) *Young People, Housing and Social Policy.* London: Routledge.

Biehal, N., Clayden, J. and Byford, S. (2000) *Home or Away? Supporting Young People and Families.* London: National Children's Bureau.

Biehal, N., Clayden, J., Stein, M. and Wade, J. (1995) *Moving On: Young People and Leaving Care Schemes.* London: HMSO.

Bilson, A. and Thorpe, D. (1988) *Child Care Careers and Their Management.* Fife: Research Development and Information Unit.

Birch, D. and Taylor, C. (2003) '"People like us?": Responding to allegations of past abuse in care.' *Criminal Law Review,* December, 823–49.

Borland, M., Pearson, C., Hill, M., Tisdall, K. and Bloomfield, I. (1998) *Education and Care Away from Home: A Review of Research, Policy and Practice.* Edinburgh: Scottish Council for Research in Education (SCRE).

Bowlby, J. (1946) *Forty-Four Juvenile Thieves: Their Characters and Home-Life.* London: Baillière.

Bowlby, J. (1951) *Maternal Care and Mental Health.* A Report Prepared on Behalf of the World Health Organisation as a Contribution to the United Nations Programme for the Welfare of Homeless Children. Geneva: World Health Organisation.

Bowlby, J. (1969) *Attachment and Loss,* Volume 1. New York: Basic Books.

Bowlby, J., Fry, S. and Ainsworth, M. (1965) *Child Care and the Growth of Love.* Harmondsworth: Penguin.

Braithwaite, J. (1989) *Crime, Shame and Reintegration.* Cambridge: Cambridge University Press.

British Society of Criminology (2003) *Code of Ethics for Researchers in the Field of Criminology.* Revised by L. Gelsthorpe, B. Williams, R. Tarling and D. Wall. www.britsoccrim.org/ethics.htm

Broad, B. (1998) *Young People Leaving Care: Life After the Children Act 1989.* London: Jessica Kingsley Publishers.

Broad, B. (ed) (2001) *Kinship Care: The Placement Choice for Children and Young People.* Lyme Regis: Russell House.

Broad, B. (2003) 'Young people leaving care: The impact of the Children (Leaving Care) Act 2000.' *ChildRight, 199,* 16–18.

Bullock, R. (1990) 'The implications of recent child care research findings for foster care.' In M. Hill (ed) (1999) *Signposts in Fostering: Policy, Practice and Research Finding.* London: BAAF.

Bullock, R., Little, M. and Millham, S. (1993) *Residential Care for Children: A Review of the Research.* London: HMSO.

Burgess, R.G. (1984) *In the Field: An Introduction to Field Research.* London: Allen & Unwin.

Butler, I. and Drakeford, M. (2001) 'Tough enough? Youth justice under New Labour.' *Probation Journal, 48,* 2, 119–124.

Carlen, P. (1987) 'Out of care, into custody.' In P. Carlen and A. Worrall (eds) *Gender, Crime and Justice.* Milton Keynes: Oxford University Press.

Children and Young People's Unit (2001) *Tomorrow's Future: Building a Strategy for Children and Young People.* London: Children and Young People's Unit.

Cliffe, D. and Berridge, D. (1991) *Closing Children's Homes: An End to Residential Childcare?* London: National Children's Bureau.

Coles, B., Rugg, J. and Seavers, J. (1999) 'Young adults living in the parental home: The implications of extended youth transitions for housing and social policy.' In J. Rugg (ed) *Young People, Housing and Social Policy.* London: Routledge.

Collins, M.E., Schwartz, I.M. and Epstein, I. (2001) 'Risk factors for adult imprisonment in a sample of youth released from residential child care.' *Children and Youth Services Review, 23,* 3, 203–226.

Colton, M. (2002) 'Factors associated with abuse in residential child care institutions.' *Children and Society, 16,* 33–44.

Communities that Care (2001) *Risk and Protective Factors Associated with Youth Crime and Effective Interventions to Prevent It.* London: Youth Justice Board.

Corby, B., Doig, A. and Roberts, V. (2001) *Public Inquiries into Abuse of Children in Residential Care.* London: Jessica Kingsley Publishers.

Cornish, D. and Clarke, R. (1975) *Residential Care and its Effects on Juvenile Delinquency.* London: HMSO.

Davies, C., Archer, S., Hicks, L. and Little, M. (1998) *Caring For Children Away From Home: Messages From Research.* London: John Wiley and Department of Health.

Department for Education and Employment and Department of Health (2000) *Guidance on the Education of Children and Young People in Public Care.* London: The Stationery Office.

Department for Education and Skills (2003a) *Children in Need in England: Preliminary Results of a Survey of Activity and Expenditure as Reported by Local Authority Social Services' Children and Families Teams for a Survey Week in February 2003.* London: Department for Education and Skills.

Department for Education and Skills (2003b) *Children Accommodated in Secure Units, Year Ending 31 March 2003: England and Wales.* London: Department for Education and Skills.

Department for Education and Skills (2003c) *Statistics of Education: Care Leavers 2002–2003, England.* London: National Statistics.

Department for Education and Skills (2003d) *Every Child Matters.* Cm. 5860. Norwich: The Stationery Office.

Department of Health (1998a) *Quality Protects – Transforming Children's Services.* London: Department of Health.

Department of Health (1998b) *Modernising Social Services.* Cm. 4169. London: The Stationery Office.

Department of Health (1999) *The Government's Objectives for Children's Social Services.* London: The Stationery Office.

Department of Health (2000) 'Educational qualifications of care leavers, year ending 31 March 2000: England.' *Statistical Bulletin 2000/25.* London: Department of Health.

Department of Health (2001a) *Outcome Indicators for Looked After Children: Year Ending 30 September 2000.* London: Department of Health.

Department of Health (2001b) 'Children's homes at 31 March 2000, England.' *Statistical Bulletin 2001/9.* London: Department of Health.

Department of Health (2001c) *Children (Leaving Care) Act 2000: Regulations and Guidance.* Available at www.dfes.gov.uk/qualityprotects/

Department of Health (2002a) *Children's Homes: National Minimum Standards and Children's Homes Regulations.* London: The Stationery Office.

Department of Health (2002b) *Fostering Services: National Minimum Standards and Fostering Services Regulations.* London: The Stationery Office.

Department of Health (2002c) *National Standards for the Provision of Children's Advocacy Services.* London: Department of Health.

Department of Health (2002d) *Choice Protects Update Bulletin No. 1* (November). London: Department of Health.

Department of Health (2003a) *Outcome Indicators for Looked-After Children, Twelve months to 30 September 2002, England.* London: Department of Health.

Department of Health (2003b) *Children Looked After by Local Authorities, Year Ending 31 March 2002, England, AF 02/12.* London: Department of Health.

Department of Health (2003c) *Choice Protects Objectives: Foster Care.* Available at www.dfes.gov.uk/choiceprotects/

Dobson, R. (2000) 'Childhood betrayed.' *Independent on Sunday,* 20 February, p.16.

Dodd, T. and Hunter, P. (1992) *The National Prison Survey 1991: A Report to the Home Office of a Study of Prisoners in England and Wales carried out by the Social Survey Division of OPCS.* London: HMSO.

Downes, C. (1992) *Separation Revisited.* Aldershot: Ashgate.

Dumaret, A., Coppel-Batsch and Couraud, S. (1997) 'Adult outcome of children reared for long-term periods in foster families.' *Child Abuse and Neglect, 21,* 10, 911–27.

Dunlop, A. (1974) *The Approved School Experience.* London: HMSO.

Dyer, C. (2002) 'Court upholds rights of jailed youngsters.' *The Guardian,* 30 November.

Emler, N. and Reicher, S. (1995) *Adolescence and Delinquency.* Oxford: Blackwell.

Farrington, D.P. (1986) 'Stepping stones to adult criminal careers.' In D. Olweus, J. Block and M. Radke-Yarrow (eds) *Development of Antisocial and Prosocial Behavior.* Orlando: Academic Press.

Farrington, D.P. and Painter, K. (2004) *Gender Differences in Risk Factors for Offending.* Home Office Research Findings 196. London: Home Office.

Ferguson, T. (1966) *Children in Care – and After.* Oxford: Oxford University Press.

Flood-Page, C., Campbell, S., Harrington, V. and Miller, J. (2000) *Youth Crime: Findings from the 1998/1999 Youth Lifestyles Survey.* Home Office Research Study 209. London: Home Office.

Frost, N., Mills, S. and Stein, M. (1999) *Understanding Residential Child Care.* Aldershot: Ashgate.

Garland, D. (2001) *The Culture of Control: Crime and Social Order in Contemporary Society.* Oxford: Oxford University Press.

George, M. (2002) 'Poor planning.' *Guardian* 'Society', 20 February, p.104.

Gilligan, R. (2001) *Promoting Resilience: A Resource Guide on Working with Children in the Care System.* London: BAAF.

Glueck, S. and Glueck, E. (1950) Unravelling Juvenile Delinquency. Cambridge, MA: Harvard University Press. Cited in R.J. Sampson and J.H. Laub (1993) *Crime in the Making: Pathways and Turning Points Through Life.* Cambridge, MA: Harvard University Press.

Goddard, J. (2000) 'Research review: The education of looked after children.' *Child and Family Social Work, 5,* 1, 79–86.

Goffman, E. (1961) *Asylums: Essays on the Social Situation of Mental Patients and Other Inmates.* New York: Doubleday.

Goldson, B. (2001) 'A rational youth justice? Some critical reflections on the research, policy and practice relation.' *Probation Journal, 48,* 2, 76–85.

Goldson, B. (2002a) *Vulnerable Inside: Children in Secure and Penal Settings.* London: The Children's Society.

Goldson, B. (2002b) 'New Labour, social justice and children: Political calculation and the deserving–undeserving schism.' *British Journal of Social Work, 32,* 683–95.

Goldson, B. and Peters, E. (2000) *Tough Justice: Responding to Children in Trouble.* London: The Children's Society.

Gottfredson, M.R. and Hirschi, T. (1990) *A General Theory of Crime.* Stanford, CA: Stanford University Press.

Graham, J. and Bowling, B. (1995) *Young People and Crime.* London: Home Office.

Hagell, A. (2003) *Understanding and Challenging Youth Offending.* Quality Protects Research Briefing No 8. London: Department of Health.

Haines, K. and Drakeford, M. (1998) *Young People and Youth Justice.* Basingstoke: Macmillan.

Hansard (2003) Edward Garnier, MP, on allegations of past abuse in children's homes. *Hansard: House of Commons, June 19 2003,* Cm. 554. London: The Stationery Office.

Harris, R. and Timms, N. (1993) *Secure Accommodation in Child Care: Between Hospital and Prison or Thereabouts?* London: Routledge.

Hayslett-McCall, K. and Bernard, T.J. (2002) 'Attachment, masculinity and self-control: A theory of male crime rates.' *Theoretical Criminology, 6,* 1, 5–33.

Hazel, N., Hagell, A., Liddle, M., Archer, D., Grimshaw, R. and King, J. (2002) *Detention and Training: Assessment of the Detention and Training Order and its Impact on the Secure Estate Across England and Wales.* London: Youth Justice Board.

Heath, A.F., Colton, M.J. and Aldgate, J. (1994) 'Failure to escape: A longitudinal study of foster children's educational attainment.' *British Journal of Social Work, 24,* 241–60.

Her Majesty's Chief Inspector of Prisons (1999) *HM Young Offender Institution and Remand Centre Feltham: Report of an Unannounced Full Inspection: 30 November to 4 December 1998.* London: Home Office.

Hirschi, T. (1969) *Causes of Delinquency.* Berkeley: University of California Press.

Home Office (1998) *Supporting Families: A Discussion Document.* London: Home Office.

Home Office (2003a) *Prison Statistics: England and Wales 2001.* Cm. 5730. Norwich: The Stationery Office.

Home Office (2003b) *Youth Justice – The Next Steps.* London: Home Office.

Home Office (2003c) *Respect and Responsibility: Taking a Stand Against Anti-Social Behaviour.* Cm. 5778. Norwich: The Stationery Office.

Home Office (2003d) *Criminal Statistics: England and Wales 2002.* Cm. 6054. Norwich: HMSO.

Hough, M., Jacobson, J. and Millie, A. (2003) *The Decision to Imprison: Sentencing and the Prison Population.* London: Prison Reform Trust.

Howard League for Penal Reform (1995) *Banged Up, Beaten Up, Cutting Up.* London: Howard League for Penal Reform.

Howard League for Penal Reform (2001) *Suicide and Self-Harm Prevention: Repetitive Self-Harm Among Women and Girls in Prison.* London: Howard League for Penal Reform.

Howe, D. (1995) *Attachment Theory for Social Work Practice.* London: Macmillan.

Howe, D., Brandon, M., Hinings, D. and Schofield, G. (1999) *Attachment Theory, Child Maltreatment and Family Support: A Practice and Assessment Model.* London: Macmillan.

Jackson, S. and Martin, P.Y. (1998) 'Surviving the care system: Education and resilience.' *Journal of Adolescence, 21,* 5, 569–83.

Jackson, S. and Sachdev, D. (2001) *Better Education, Better Futures: Research, Practice and the Views of Young People in Public Care.* Ilford, Essex: Barnardo's.

Jackson, S. and Thomas, N. (1999) *On the Move Again? What Works in Creating Stability for Looked After Children.* Ilford, Essex: Barnardo's.

Jonson-Reid, M. and Barth, R.P. (2000) 'From placement to prison: The path to adolescent incarceration from child welfare supervised foster or group care.' *Children and Youth Services Review, 22,* 7, 493–516.

Kahan, B. (1979) *Growing up in Care.* Oxford: Basil Blackwell.

Laming, Lord (2003) *The Victoria Climbie Inquiry: Report of an Inquiry by Lord Laming.* Cm. 5730. Norwich: The Stationery Office.

Land, H. (2002) *Meeting the Child Poverty Challenge.* London: The Daycare Trust.

Laub, J.H. and Sampson, R.J. (1994) 'Unemployment, marital discord and deviant behaviour: The long-term correlates of childhood misbehaviour.' In T. Hirschi and M.R. Gottfredson (eds) *The Generality of Deviance.* New Brunswick: Transaction Publishers.

Laub, J.H., Nagin, D.S. and Sampson, R.J. (1998) 'Trajectories of change incriminal offending: Good marriages and the desistance process.' *American Sociological Review, 63,* 225–38.

Lee, R.M. and Renzetti, C.M. (1993) 'The problem of researching sensitive topics: An overview and introduction.' In C.M. Renzetti and R.M. Lee (eds) *Researching Sensitive Topics.* Newbury Park: Sage Publications.

Lindsay, M. (1996) *Towards a Theory of 'careism' – Discrimination Against Young People in Care*. Paper given at the International Conference on Residential Child Care, Glasgow, September.

Lipsey, M. (1995) 'What do we learn from 400 research studies on the effectiveness of treatment with juvenile delinquents?.' In J. Maguire (ed) *What Works: Reducing Reoffending*. Chichester: Wiley.

Lord Chancellor's Department (1999) 'Human Rights Act – How it will help for children.' News release, 26 January 1999. Available at www.dca.gov.uk/hract

Lyon, J., Dennison, C. and Wilson, A. (2000) *'Tell Them so They Listen': Focus Group Research with Young People in Custody*. Home Office Research Study No. 201. London: Home Office.

Main, M. (1991) 'Metacognitive knowledge, metacognitive monitoring, and singular (coherent) vs. multiple (incoherent) model of attachment.' In C.M. Parkes, J. Stevenson-Hinde and P. Marris (eds) *Attachment Across the Life Cycle*. London: Routledge.

Maruna, S. (2001) *Making Good: How Ex-Convicts Reform and Rebuild Their Lives*. Washington DC: American Psychological Association.

Mason, J. (1996) *Qualitative Researching*. London: Sage Publications.

McCarthy, P., Laing, K. and Walker, J. (2004) *Offenders of the Future? Assessing the Risk of Children and Young People Becoming Involved in Criminal or Antisocial Behaviour*. Department for Education and Skills, Research Report 545. London: Department for Education and Skills.

McMahon, J. and Clay-Warner, J. (2002) 'Child abuse and future criminality: The role of social service placement, family disorganization, and gender.' *Journal of Interpersonal Violence, 17*, 9, 1002–1019.

Millham, S., Bullock, R. and Cherret, P. (1975) *After Grace – Teeth*. London: Chaucer Publishing Co. Ltd.

Minty, B. (1999) 'Annotation: Outcomes in long-term foster family care.' *Journal of Child Psychology and Psychiatry, 40*, 7, 991–9.

Minty, B. and Ashcroft, C. (1987) *Child Care and Adult Crime*. Manchester: Manchester University Press.

Mitchell, J. (1983) 'Case study and situational analysis.' *Sociological Review, 31*, 187–211.

MORI (Market and Opinion Research International) (2004) *MORI Youth Survey 2004*. London: Youth Justice Board.

Morris, J. (2000) *Having Someone Who Cares? Barriers to Change in the Public Care of Children*. London: National Children's Bureau.

Munro, E. (2001) 'Empowering looked-after children.' *Child and Family Social Work, 6*, 129–37.

NACRO (National Association for the Care and Resettlement of Offenders) (2003a) *A Failure of Justice: Reducing Child Imprisonment*. London: NACRO.

NACRO (National Association for the Care and Resettlement of Offenders) (2003b) *Reducing Offending by Looked after Children: A Good Practice Guide*. London: NACRO.

National Children's Bureau (1995) *Safe to Let Out?: The Current and Future Uses of Secure Accommodation for Children and Young People*. London: National Children's Bureau.

Oakley, A. (1999) 'People's ways of knowing: gender and methodology.' In S. Hood, B. Mayall and S. Oliver (eds) *Critical Issues in Social Research: Power and Prejudice.* Buckingham: OUP.

O'Neill, T. (2001) *Children in Secure Accommodation: A Gendered Exploration of Locked Institutional Care for Children in Trouble.* London: Jessica Kingsley Publishers.

Parkes, C.M., Stevenson-Hinde, J. and Marris, P. (eds) *(1991) Attachment Across the Life Cycle.* London: Routledge.

Pawson, R. and Tilley, N. (1997) *Realistic Evaluation.* London: Sage Publications.

Polsky, H. (1962) *Cottage Six.* New York: Sage Publications.

Quinton, D. and Rutter, M. (1988) *Parenting Breakdown: The Making and Breaking of Inter-Generational Links.* Aldershot: Avebury.

Reinharz, S. (1992) *Feminist Methods in Social Research.* Oxford: Oxford University Press.

Rutter, M. (1971) 'Parent–child separation: Psychological effects on the children.' *Journal of Child Psychology and Psychiatry, 12,* 233–60.

Rutter, M., Giller, H. and Hagell, A. (1998) *Antisocial Behavior by Young People.* Cambridge: Cambridge University Press.

Sampson, R. and Laub, J. (1993) *Crime in the Making: Pathways and Turning Points Through Life.* London: Harvard University Press.

Sampson, R.J. and Laub, J.H. (1995) 'Understanding variability in lives through time: Contributions of life-course criminology.' *Studies on Crime and Crime Prevention, 4,* 143–58.

Sampson, R.J. and Laub, J.H. (1996) 'Socioeconomic achievement in the life course of disadvantaged men: Military service as a turning point, circa 1940–1965.' *American Sociological Review, 61,* 3, 347–67.

Schofield, G. (2001) 'Resilience and family placement: A lifespan perspective.' *Adoption and Fostering, 25,* 3, 6–19.

Schofield, G. (2003) *Part of the Family: Pathways Through Foster Care.* London: BAAF.

Schofield, G., Beek, M., Sargent, K. and Thoburn, J. (2000) *Growing Up in Foster Care.* London: BAAF.

Scholte, E.M., Colton, M., Casas, F., Drakeford, M., Roberts, S. and Williams, M. (1999) 'Perceptions of stigma and user involvement in child welfare services.' *British Journal of Social Work, 29,* 3, 373–91.

SEU (Social Exclusion Unit) (1998) *Truancy and School Exclusion.* London: Social Exclusion Unit.

SEU (Social Exclusion Unit) (2001) *Preventing Social Exclusion.* London: Social Exclusion Unit.

SEU (Social Exclusion Unit) (2003) *A Better Education for Children in Care.* London: Social Exclusion Unit.

Shaw, C. (1998) *Remember My Messages.* Brighton: The Who Cares? Trust.

Silverman, D. (2000) *Doing Qualitative Research: A Practical Handbook.* London: Sage Publications.

Silverman, D. (2001) *Interpreting Qualitative Data: Methods for Analysing Talk, Text and Interaction.* Second edition. London: Sage Publications.

Sinclair, I. and Gibbs, I. (1998) *Children's Homes: A Study in Diversity.* Chichester: John Wiley.

Sinclair, I. and Wilson, K. (2003) 'Matches and mismatches: The contribution of carers and children to the success of foster placements.' *British Journal of Social Work, 33,* 871–84.

Sinclair, I., Gibbs, I. and Wilson, K. (2000) *Supporting Foster Placements: Reports One and Two.* York: Social Work Research and Development Unit.

Smith, D. (1999) 'Social work with young people in trouble: Memory and prospect.' In B. Goldson (ed) *Youth Justice: Contemporary Policy and Practice.* Aldershot: Ashgate.

Smith, D. (2000) 'Learning from the Scottish juvenile justice system.' *Probation Journal, 47,* 1, 12–17.

Smith, D. (2003) 'New Labour and youth justice.' *Children and Society, 17,* 226–35.

Social Services Inspectorate (1997) *When Leaving Home is also Leaving Care: An Inspection of Services for Young People Leaving Care.* Wetherby: Department of Health.

Soothill, K. (ed) *(1999) Criminal Conversations: An Anthology of the Work of Tony Parker.* London: Routledge.

Stanley, L. and Wise, S. (1993) *Breaking Out Again.* London: Routledge.

Stein, M. (1994) 'Leaving care, education and career trajectories.' *Oxford Review of Education, 20,* 3, 349–60.

Stein, M. (1997) *What Works in Leaving Care?* Barkingside, Essex: Barnados.

Stein, M. and Carey, K. (1986) *Leaving Care.* Oxford: Basil Blackwell.

Stein, M. and Wade, J. (2000) *Helping Care Leavers: Problems and Strategic Responses: Executive Summary.* London: Department of Health.

Stewart, J., Smith, D., Stewart, G. with C. Fullwood (1994) *Understanding Offending Behaviour.* Harlow, Essex: Longman Group Limited.

Taylor, C. (2001) 'The relationship between social and self-control: Tracing Hirschi's criminological career.' *Theoretical Criminology, 5,* 3, 369–88.

Taylor, C. (2003) 'Justice for looked after children?' *Probation Journal, 50,* 3, 239–51.

Taylor, C. (2004) 'Social work and looked after children.' In D.B. Smith (ed) *Social Work and Evidence-Based Practice.* London: Jessica Kingsley Publishers.

Thorpe, D.H., Smith, D., Green, C.J. and Paley, J.H. (1980) *Out of Care.* London: George Allen & Unwin.

Tizard, B. (1986) *The Care of Young Children: Implications of Recent Research.* London: Thomas Coram Research Unit.

Travis, A. (2002) '10-year-old offenders to be sent to foster homes.' *Guardian,* 15 November.

Triseliotis, J., Borland, M., Hill, M. and Lambert, L. (1995) *Teenagers and the Social Work Services.* London: HMSO.

Trotter, C. (1999) *Working with Involuntary Clients.* London: Sage Publications.

United Nations (1989) *The United Nations Convention on the Rights of the Child.* New York: United Nations.

United Nations Committee on the Rights of the Child (2002) *Consideration of Reports Submitted by States Parties Under Article 44 of the Convention. Concluding Observations: United Kingdom of Great Britain and Northern Ireland.* Geneva: Office of the United Nations High Commissioner for Human Rights.

Utting, W. (1991) *Children in the Public Care.* London: HMSO.

Utting, W. (1997) *People Like Us: The Report of the Review of the Safeguards for Children Living Away From Home.* London: The Stationery Office.

Vernon, J. (2000) *Audit and Assessment of Leaving Care Services in London*. London: Department of Health and Rough Sleepers Unit.

Wade, J. (2003) *Leaving Care.* Quality Protects Research Briefing No. 7. London: Department of Health.

Walker, M., Hill, M. and Triseliotis, J. (2002) *Testing the Limits of Foster Care: Fostering as an Alternative to Secure Accommodation.* London: BAAF.

Ward, H. and Skuse, T. (2001) 'Performance targets and stability of placements for children long looked after away from home.' *Children and Society, 15,* 333–46.

Ward, J., Henderson, Z. and Pearson, G. (2003) *One Problem Among Many: Drug Use among Care-Leavers in Transition to Independent Living.* Home Office Research Study 260. London: Home Office.

Warner, N. (1992) *Choosing with Care: The Report of the Committee of Inquiry into the Selection, Development and Management of Staff in Children's Homes.* London: HMSO.

Waterhouse, R. (2000) *Lost in Care: Report of the Tribunal of Inquiry into the Abuse of Children in Care in the Former County Council Areas of Gwynedd and Clwyd since 1974.* London: HMSO.

Whitaker, D., Archer, L. and Hicks, L. (1998) *Working in Children's Homes: Challenges and Complexities.* Chichester: John Wiley.

Wilson, J. and Herrnstein, R. (1985) *Crime And Human Nature.* New York: Simon & Schuster. Cited in M.R. Gottfredson and T. Hirschi (1990) *A General Theory of Crime.* Stanford, CA: Stanford University Press.

Wilson, K., Sinclair, I., Taylor, C., Pithouse, A. and Sellick, C. (2004) *Fostering Success: An Exploration of the Research Literature in Foster Care.* Report for the Social Care Institute of Excellence. London: SCIE.

Worrall, A. (2001) 'Girls at risk? Reflections on changing attitudes to young women's offending.' *Probation Journal, 48,* 2, 86–92.

Youth Justice Board (2003a) *Youth Justice Board for England and Wales: About Us.* Available at www.youth-justice-board.gov.uk/YouthJusticeBoard

Youth Justice Board (2003b) *Youth Justice Board News.* Issue 16, February. London: Youth Justice Board.

Subject index

abuse
    in care settings 15, 21, 24, 39, 43–4
    as reason for admittance to care 23,
        32, 84, 90
    see also alcohol abuse; drug abuse;
        physical abuse; sexual abuse
accommodation 151
    for care-leavers 47–8, 161–6, 170,
        183
    secure 25–6, 42
    see also foyer initiative; hostels;
        semi-independence units;
        supported lodgings
achievements, educational 27–9, 126–7
    lower expectations of children in care
        45
    in prison 139–40, 182–3
    raising self-esteem 119, 145, 182
    rewarding of 183
activities, in children's homes 95–7
admission to care, reasons for 25, 32, 50,
    80, 128–9
adulthood
    convictions, link to being in care
        33–4
    outcomes 68, 185
    transition to 30, 47–8, 63, 183
aftercare support 154–8, 183–4
    age, of interviewees in study 73–4
alcohol abuse 86, 91, 156–8
    link to crime 169, 178
    parental 90–1, 128, 158
antisocial behaviour 32, 52–3, 62–3, 65,
    83
assault, of staff in children's homes 88–9
Asylums (Goffman) 75–6
attachment 67–8, 120–1
    as deterrent to criminal career 61,
        101–2, 113
    developed in child-care settings 68,
        92–4
    different levels of 64–5, 68

    effect on educational achievement
        145
    formed in later life 63, 64, 121
    to foster carers 102–6, 108, 176–7
    to institutional way of life 121–2,
        167
    and positive self-image 110–11
    and resilience 66, 120
    theories of 57–61
attitudes, towards children in care 26–7

'baggage of disadvantage' 14, 34, 58, 64,
    101
Banged Up, Beaten Up, Cutting Up (Howard
    League) 50
'beyond parental control' 23, 32, 42
bonding, parent–child 58–9
budgeting, learning about 30, 151–2,
    154
bullying
    in prisons 50
    in residential care homes 86, 87, 98,
        175
    at school 117, 118, 136, 137

care orders 16, 32, 41–2
Care Standards Act (2000) 43
care-leavers
    accommodation for 47, 161–6
    aftercare support 154–8
    age of 29, 46, 47, 150–1, 162
    difficulties faced by 29–30, 167
    emotional needs of 158–60
    employment assistance for 47
    homelessness of 30, 47–8, 166
    lack of support for 166–9
    local authority duties towards 46
    research on 29–30
    see also aftercare support; independent
        life
caring adults, importance of 85, 92–3,
    95, 114–16, 176–7
Caring for Children Away From Home (Davies
    et al.) 25
change, potential for 63, 66–7, 68

Author index

Ainsworth, M.D. 58, 59, 60, 103
Aldgate, J. 27
Archer, L. 95
Ashcroft, C. 33–4, 65

Barnes, V. 162
Barth, R.P. 35
Bernard, T.J. 60, 186
Berridge, D. 14, 25, 28, 45, 91, 133
Biehal, N. 27, 29, 47
Bilson, A. 22
Birch, D. 15, 180
Borland, M. 28
Bowlby, J. 33, 58–61
Bowling, B. 22
Braithwaite, J. 27, 62
British Society of Criminology 71
Broad, B. 21, 30, 37, 46, 153, 159, 169, 170, 187
Brodie, I. 28, 45, 91
Bullock, R. 23, 24, 26, 37
Burgess, R.G. 70
Butler, I. 50
Byford, S. 27

Carlen, P. 34, 122, 168
Cherret, P. 24
Children and Young People's Unit 49
Clarke, R. 24, 33, 100
Clayden, J. 27
Clay-Warner, J. 36
Cliffe, D. 25, 133
Coles, B. 47
Collins, M.E. 36
Colton, M. 15, 27, 43, 55, 175
Communities that Care 28
Coppel-Batsch, M. 23
Corby, B. 79
Cornish, D. 24, 33, 100
Couraud, S. 23

Davies, C. 21, 25, 79, 98

Dennison, C. 31
Department for Education and Employment 27, 44, 45
Department of Health 13, 21, 23, 27, 28, 31, 32, 39, 43, 44, 45, 51, 56, 79, 90, 99, 101, 125, 129, 132, 136, 144, 149, 150, 151, 153, 168, 181
Dobson, R. 26
Dodd, T. 31
Doig, A. 79
Downes, C. 64, 176
Drakeford, M. 50
Dumaret, A. 23, 33
Dunlop, A. 24, 33
Dyer, C. 50

Emler, N. 70
Epstein, I. 36

Farrington, D.P. 36, 50
Ferguson, T. 33
Flood-Page, C. 120
Frost, N. 25, 98–9
Fry, S. 58

Garland, D. 55
George, M. 40
Giller, H. 14
Gilligan, R. 66, 68, 180
Glueck, E. 63
Glueck, S. 63
Goddard, J. 28, 30, 44
Goffman, E. 75
Goldson, B. 26, 39, 41, 42, 49, 50, 54, 139, 184
Gottfredson, M.R. 61–2, 63, 175
Graham, J. 22

Hagell, A. 14, 186
Haines, K. 50
Hansard (House of Commons) 79
Harris, R. 25, 42
Hayslett-McCall, K. 60
Hazel, N. 13, 31
Heath, A.F. 27, 47
Henderson, Z. 120